KAHLIL GIBRAN'S
The Prophet
A GRAPHIC NOVEL

ADAPTED & ILLUSTRATED BY PETE KATZ

San Diego, California

Canterbury Classics
An imprint of Printers Row Publishing Group
10350 Barnes Canyon Road, Suite 100, San Diego, CA 92121
www.canterburyclassicsbooks.com • mail@canterburyclassicsbooks.com

Correspondence concerning the content of this book should be sent to Canterbury Classics, Editorial Department, at the above address. Author, illustration, and rights inquiries should be sent to Quarto Publishing plc, 6 Blundell Street, London, N7 9BH, www.quartoknows.com.

Publisher: Peter Norton • Associate Publisher: Ana Parker
Editor: Dan Mansfield
Senior Product Manager: Kathryn C. Dalby

Produced by Quarto Publishing plc
Publisher: James Evans
Editorial Director: Isheeta Mustafi
Managing Editor: Jacqui Sayers
Art Director: Katherine Radcliffe
Development Editor: Abbie Sharman
Project Editor: David Price-Goodfellow, D & N Publishing
Illustrator and Script Writer: Pete Katz

Library of Congress Control Number: 2020938151

ISBN: 978-1-64517-242-0

Printed in China

24 23 22 21 20   1 2 3 4 5

Contents

Jibrān Khalīl Jibrān, or Kahlil Gibran as he is known in English, was born in 1883, in a village in Lebanon to a Maronite (Eastern Catholic) family. His parents often welcomed houseguests of various faiths, and Gibran's openness and religious tolerance may well have germinated here. He emigrated to the United States in 1895 with his mother and siblings; his creative abilities were noticed by his Boston teachers and Fred Holland Day, a photographer and publisher. At the age of fifteen, Gibran was sent back to his homeland, where he studied at the Collège de la Sagesse in Beirut.

He returned to Boston in 1902 on the death of his youngest sister. Tragically, within a year he also lost his mother and older brother. But Gibran kept working and in 1905 his drawings were exhibited for the first time and his first Arabic book was published. Gibran studied art in Paris from 1908 to 1910, and it was during this time that he became involved with Syrian political theorists and became a voice for the anti-Ottoman rebellion—even having some writings banned by the Ottoman authorities.

Gibran settled in New York in 1911 and his first English book, *The Madman*, was published in 1918. He was reported to have started work on *The Prophet* in the same year, and it was eventually published in 1923. In the book's first year it sold more than a thousand copies. This doubled in 1924, and doubled again in 1925. By the time of Gibran's death in 1931, it had also been translated into French and German. Annual sales reached 12,000 in 1935, which increased to 240,000 by 1965. The millionth copy was sold in 1957. *The Prophet* has since been translated into over 100 languages, making it one of the most translated books in existence, and since its first publication it has never been out of print.

Gibran was not only inspired by his own Catholic religion but also by Islamic mysticism, classical mythology, romanticism, symbolism, and surrealism. This broad combination of influences, Gibran's marvelous allegorical style, and the book's message of peace, love, empathy, and religious unity appealed to the New Age and counterculture movements of the 1960s, causing a rise in its popularity that spread to the wider world and has continued to this day. Elvis Presley, John Lennon, and David Bowie are all cited as owning a copy.

There have been a few adaptations of *The Prophet* over the years, including a parody, *The Profit (Albran's Serial)*, published in 1973, a musical interpretation released on Atlantic Records in 1974, and an animated film produced by Salma Hayek in 2014. In our adaptation, we wanted not only to illustrate Gibran's beautiful poetry but also to show *The Prophet*'s positive impact on its millions of readers, which is why we have added the narrative with Al and her ailing father. We have kept the poetry text in its original form but have adjusted the order of the poems, so that their individual subject matter follows a similar pattern to Al's narrative. We have also listed the poems individually in the contents so that your favorite pieces are easy to find.

In no way do we think *The Prophet* needed enhancing, but we hope that this edition may reignite your love for the book. Or if you've always wanted to read Gibran but have never gotten around to it, then maybe this version will finally draw you in. And if that's the case, sit back, relax, and enjoy.

"For in the dew of little things the heart finds its morning and is refreshed."

Gibran, *The Prophet: A Graphic Novel*, page 79

Dramatis Personae

The Prophet, Almustafa, who has been stranded in Orphalese for twelve years.

Almitra, the mysterious Seeress, is the Prophet's closest friend in Orphalese.

Al, a successful contemporary artist who is struggling to cope with her father's long-term hospitalization.

Yusef, Al's father, who has been in the hospital for three months.

Andrew, a nurse, who has known Al for years and is her best friend.

Kim, a PR consultant. She is another close friend and confidant of Al.

Part 1

THE CITY IS CHILLY THIS EVENING, AS AL MAKES THE NOW VERY FAMILIAR JOURNEY TO VISIT HER SICK FATHER.

The Prophet

ALMUSTAFA, THE CHOSEN AND THE BELOVED, WHO WAS A DAWN UNTO HIS OWN DAY, HAD WAITED TWELVE YEARS IN THE CITY OF ORPHALESE FOR HIS SHIP THAT WAS TO RETURN AND BEAR HIM BACK TO THE ISLE OF HIS BIRTH.

AND IN THE TWELFTH YEAR, ON THE SEVENTH DAY OF IELOOL, THE MONTH OF REAPING, HE CLIMBED THE HILL WITHOUT THE CITY WALLS AND LOOKED SEAWARD; AND HE BEHELD HIS SHIP COMING WITH THE MIST. THEN THE GATES OF HIS HEART WERE FLUNG OPEN, AND HIS JOY FLEW FAR OVER THE SEA. AND HE CLOSED HIS EYES AND PRAYED IN THE SILENCES OF HIS SOUL.

YET I CANNOT TARRY LONGER. THE SEA THAT CALLS ALL THINGS UNTO HER CALLS ME, AND I MUST EMBARK. FOR TO STAY, THOUGH THE HOURS BURN IN THE NIGHT, IS TO FREEZE AND CRYSTALLIZE AND BE BOUND IN A MOULD.

FAIN WOULD I TAKE WITH ME ALL THAT IS HERE. BUT HOW SHALL I?

A VOICE CANNOT CARRY THE TONGUE AND THE LIPS THAT GAVE IT WINGS. ALONE MUST IT SEEK THE ETHER.

AND ALONE AND WITHOUT HIS NEST SHALL THE EAGLE FLY ACROSS THE SUN.

NOW WHEN HE REACHED THE FOOT OF THE HILL, HE TURNED AGAIN TOWARDS THE SEA, AND HE SAW HIS SHIP APPROACHING THE HARBOUR, AND UPON HER PROW THE MARINERS, THE MEN OF HIS OWN LAND. AND HIS SOUL CRIED OUT TO THEM, AND HE SAID:

SONS OF MY ANCIENT MOTHER, YOU RIDERS OF THE TIDES, HOW OFTEN HAVE YOU SAILED IN MY DREAMS. AND NOW YOU COME IN MY AWAKENING, WHICH IS MY DEEPER DREAM.

READY AM I TO GO, AND MY EAGERNESS WITH SAILS FULL SET AWAITS THE WIND.

ONLY ANOTHER BREATH WILL I BREATHE IN THIS STILL AIR, ONLY ANOTHER LOVING LOOK CAST BACKWARD, AND THEN I SHALL STAND AMONG YOU, A SEAFARER AMONG SEAFARERS.

AND YOU, VAST SEA, SLEEPING MOTHER, WHO ALONE ARE PEACE AND FREEDOM TO THE RIVER AND THE STREAM, ONLY ANOTHER WINDING WILL THIS STREAM MAKE, ONLY ANOTHER MURMUR IN THIS GLADE, AND THEN SHALL I COME TO YOU, A BOUNDLESS DROP TO A BOUNDLESS OCEAN.

AND AS HE WALKED HE SAW FROM AFAR MEN AND WOMEN LEAVING THEIR FIELDS AND THEIR VINEYARDS AND HASTENING TOWARDS THE CITY GATES.

AND HE HEARD THEIR VOICES CALLING HIS NAME, AND SHOUTING FROM FIELD TO FIELD TELLING ONE ANOTHER OF THE COMING OF HIS SHIP.

AND HE SAID TO HIMSELF:

SHALL THE DAY OF PARTING BE THE DAY OF GATHERING? AND SHALL IT BE SAID THAT MY EVE WAS IN TRUTH MY DAWN?

15

AND WHAT SHALL I GIVE UNTO HIM WHO HAS LEFT HIS PLOUGH IN MIDFURROW, OR TO HIM WHO HAS STOPPED THE WHEEL OF HIS WINEPRESS?
SHALL MY HEART BECOME A TREE HEAVY-LADEN WITH FRUIT THAT I MAY GATHER AND GIVE UNTO THEM?

AND SHALL MY DESIRES FLOW LIKE A FOUNTAIN THAT I MAY FILL THEIR CUPS?
AM I A HARP THAT THE HAND OF THE MIGHTY MAY TOUCH ME, OR A FLUTE THAT HIS BREATH MAY PASS THROUGH ME?

A SEEKER OF SILENCES AM I, AND WHAT TREASURE HAVE I FOUND IN SILENCES THAT I MAY DISPENSE WITH CONFIDENCE?
IF THIS IS MY DAY OF HARVEST, IN WHAT FIELDS HAVE I SOWED THE SEED, AND IN WHAT UNREMEMBERED SEASONS?

IF THIS INDEED BE THE HOUR IN WHICH I LIFT UP MY LANTERN, IT IS NOT MY FLAME THAT SHALL BURN THEREIN.
EMPTY AND DARK SHALL I RAISE MY LANTERN, AND THE GUARDIAN OF THE NIGHT SHALL FILL IT WITH OIL AND HE SHALL LIGHT IT ALSO.

THESE THINGS HE SAID IN WORDS. BUT MUCH IN HIS HEART REMAINED UNSAID. FOR HE HIMSELF COULD NOT SPEAK HIS DEEPER SECRET.

AND OTHERS CAME ALSO AND ENTREATED HIM. BUT HE ANSWERED THEM NOT. HE ONLY BENT HIS HEAD; AND THOSE WHO STOOD NEAR SAW HIS TEARS FALLING UPON HIS BREAST.

AND HE AND THE PEOPLE PROCEEDED TOWARDS THE GREAT SQUARE BEFORE THE TEMPLE.

AND THERE CAME OUT OF THE SANCTUARY A WOMAN WHOSE NAME WAS ALMITRA. AND SHE WAS A SEERESS.

AND HE LOOKED UPON HER WITH EXCEEDING TENDERNESS, FOR IT WAS SHE WHO HAD FIRST SOUGHT AND BELIEVED IN HIM WHEN HE HAD BEEN BUT A DAY IN THEIR CITY.
AND SHE HAILED HIM, SAYING:

PROPHET OF GOD, IN QUEST OF THE UTTERMOST, LONG HAVE YOU SEARCHED THE DISTANCES FOR YOUR SHIP.

AND NOW YOUR SHIP HAS COME, AND YOU MUST NEEDS GO.

DEEP IS YOUR LONGING FOR THE LAND OF YOUR MEMORIES AND THE DWELLING-PLACE OF YOUR GREATER DESIRES; AND OUR LOVE WOULD NOT BIND YOU NOR OUR NEEDS HOLD YOU.

YET THIS WE ASK ERE YOU LEAVE US, THAT YOU SPEAK TO US AND GIVE US OF YOUR TRUTH.

AND WE WILL GIVE IT UNTO OUR CHILDREN, AND THEY UNTO THEIR CHILDREN, AND IT SHALL NOT PERISH.

IN YOUR ALONENESS YOU HAVE WATCHED WITH OUR DAYS, AND IN YOUR WAKEFULNESS YOU HAVE LISTENED TO THE WEEPING AND THE LAUGHTER OF OUR SLEEP.

NOW THEREFORE DISCLOSE US TO OURSELVES, AND TELL US ALL THAT HAS BEEN SHOWN YOU OF THAT WHICH IS BETWEEN BIRTH AND DEATH.

AND HE ANSWERED:

PEOPLE OF ORPHALESE,

OF WHAT CAN I SPEAK SAVE OF THAT WHICH IS EVEN NOW MOVING WITHIN YOUR SOULS?

THEN SAID ALMITRA,

SPEAK TO US OF LOVE.

AND HE RAISED HIS HEAD AND LOOKED UPON THE PEOPLE, AND THERE FELL A STILLNESS UPON THEM. AND WITH A GREAT VOICE HE SAID:

19

WHEN LOVE BECKONS TO YOU,
FOLLOW HIM,
THOUGH HIS WAYS ARE HARD AND STEEP.

AND WHEN HIS WINGS ENFOLD YOU
YIELD TO HIM,
THOUGH THE SWORD HIDDEN AMONG HIS
PINIONS MAY WOUND YOU.

AND WHEN HE SPEAKS TO YOU
BELIEVE IN HIM,
THOUGH HIS VOICE MAY SHATTER YOUR
DREAMS AS THE NORTH WIND LAYS
WASTE THE GARDEN.

FOR EVEN AS LOVE CROWNS YOU SO
SHALL HE CRUCIFY YOU.
EVEN AS HE IS FOR YOUR GROWTH SO IS
HE FOR YOUR PRUNING.

EVEN AS HE ASCENDS TO YOUR HEIGHT
AND CARESSES YOUR TENDEREST
BRANCHES THAT QUIVER IN THE SUN,

SO SHALL HE DESCEND TO YOUR ROOTS
AND SHAKE THEM IN THEIR CLINGING TO
THE EARTH.

LIKE SHEAVES OF CORN HE GATHERS
YOU UNTO HIMSELF.

HE THRESHES YOU TO MAKE YOU NAKED.
HE SIFTS YOU TO FREE YOU FROM YOUR
HUSKS.
HE GRINDS YOU TO WHITENESS.
HE KNEADS YOU UNTIL YOU ARE PLIANT;

AND THEN HE ASSIGNS YOU TO HIS
SACRED FIRE, THAT YOU MAY BECOME
SACRED BREAD FOR GOD'S SACRED
FEAST.

ALL THESE THINGS SHALL LOVE DO UNTO YOU THAT YOU
MAY KNOW THE SECRETS OF YOUR HEART, AND IN THAT
KNOWLEDGE BECOME A FRAGMENT OF LIFE'S HEART.

BUT IF IN YOUR FEAR YOU WOULD SEEK ONLY LOVE'S
PEACE AND LOVE'S PLEASURE,
THEN IT IS BETTER FOR YOU THAT YOU COVER YOUR
NAKEDNESS AND PASS OUT OF LOVE'S THRESHING-FLOOR,

INTO THE SEASONLESS WORLD WHERE YOU SHALL LAUGH,
BUT NOT ALL OF YOUR LAUGHTER, AND WEEP, BUT NOT
ALL OF YOUR TEARS.

LOVE GIVES NAUGHT BUT ITSELF AND TAKES NAUGHT BUT FROM ITSELF.

LOVE POSSESSES NOT NOR WOULD IT BE POSSESSED; FOR LOVE IS SUFFICIENT UNTO LOVE.

WHEN YOU LOVE YOU SHOULD NOT SAY, "GOD IS IN MY HEART," BUT RATHER, "I AM IN THE HEART OF GOD."

AND THINK NOT YOU CAN DIRECT THE COURSE OF LOVE, FOR LOVE, IF IT FINDS YOU WORTHY, DIRECTS YOUR COURSE.

LOVE HAS NO OTHER DESIRE BUT TO FULFIL ITSELF.

BUT IF YOU LOVE AND MUST NEEDS HAVE DESIRES, LET THESE BE YOUR DESIRES:

TO MELT AND BE LIKE A RUNNING BROOK THAT SINGS ITS MELODY TO THE NIGHT.
TO KNOW THE PAIN OF TOO MUCH TENDERNESS.

TO BE WOUNDED BY YOUR OWN UNDERSTANDING OF LOVE;
AND TO BLEED WILLINGLY AND JOYFULLY.

TO WAKE AT DAWN WITH A WINGED HEART AND GIVE THANKS FOR ANOTHER DAY OF LOVING;

TO REST AT THE NOON HOUR AND MEDITATE LOVE'S ECSTASY;

TO RETURN HOME AT EVENTIDE WITH GRATITUDE;

AND THEN TO SLEEP WITH A PRAYER FOR THE BELOVED IN YOUR HEART AND A SONG OF PRAISE UPON YOUR LIPS.

THEN ALMITRA SPOKE AGAIN AND SAID,
AND WHAT OF MARRIAGE, MASTER?

AND HE ANSWERED SAYING:

YOU WERE BORN TOGETHER, AND TOGETHER YOU SHALL BE FOR EVERMORE.
YOU SHALL BE TOGETHER WHEN THE WHITE WINGS OF DEATH SCATTER YOUR DAYS.
AYE, YOU SHALL BE TOGETHER EVEN IN THE SILENT MEMORY OF GOD.

BUT LET THERE BE SPACES IN YOUR TOGETHERNESS.
AND LET THE WINDS OF THE HEAVENS DANCE BETWEEN YOU.

LOVE ONE ANOTHER, BUT MAKE NOT A BOND OF LOVE: LET IT RATHER BE A MOVING SEA BETWEEN THE SHORES OF YOUR SOULS.

FILL EACH OTHER'S CUP BUT DRINK NOT FROM ONE CUP. GIVE ONE ANOTHER OF YOUR BREAD BUT EAT NOT FROM THE SAME LOAF.
SING AND DANCE TOGETHER AND BE JOYOUS, BUT LET EACH ONE OF YOU BE ALONE, EVEN AS THE STRINGS OF A LUTE ARE ALONE THOUGH THEY QUIVER WITH THE SAME MUSIC.

GIVE YOUR HEARTS, BUT NOT INTO EACH OTHER'S KEEPING. FOR ONLY THE HAND OF LIFE CAN CONTAIN YOUR HEARTS.
AND STAND TOGETHER YET NOT TOO NEAR TOGETHER: FOR THE PILLARS OF THE TEMPLE STAND APART, AND THE OAK TREE AND THE CYPRESS GROW NOT IN EACH OTHER'S SHADOW.

THEN AN OLD MAN, A KEEPER OF AN INN, SAID,
SPEAK TO US OF EATING AND DRINKING.

AND HE SAID:

WOULD THAT YOU COULD LIVE ON THE FRAGRANCE OF THE EARTH, AND LIKE AN AIR PLANT BE SUSTAINED BY THE LIGHT.

BUT SINCE YOU MUST KILL TO EAT, AND ROB THE NEWLY BORN OF ITS MOTHER'S MILK TO QUENCH YOUR THIRST, LET IT THEN BE AN ACT OF WORSHIP,

AND LET YOUR BOARD STAND AN ALTAR ON WHICH THE PURE AND THE INNOCENT OF FOREST AND PLAIN ARE SACRIFICED FOR THAT WHICH IS PURER AND STILL MORE INNOCENT IN MAN.

WHEN YOU KILL A BEAST SAY TO HIM IN YOUR HEART:

"BY THE SAME POWER THAT SLAYS YOU, I TOO AM SLAIN; AND I TOO SHALL BE CONSUMED.
FOR THE LAW THAT DELIVERED YOU INTO MY HAND SHALL DELIVER ME INTO A MIGHTIER HAND.
YOUR BLOOD AND MY BLOOD IS NAUGHT BUT THE SAP THAT FEEDS THE TREE OF HEAVEN."

AND WHEN YOU CRUSH AN APPLE WITH YOUR TEETH, SAY TO IT IN YOUR HEART:

"YOUR SEEDS SHALL LIVE IN MY BODY, AND THE BUDS OF YOUR TOMORROW SHALL BLOSSOM IN MY HEART, AND YOUR FRAGRANCE SHALL BE MY BREATH, AND TOGETHER WE SHALL REJOICE THROUGH ALL THE SEASONS."

AND IN THE AUTUMN, WHEN YOU GATHER THE GRAPES OF YOUR VINEYARDS FOR THE WINEPRESS, SAY IN YOUR HEART:

"I TOO AM A VINEYARD, AND MY FRUIT SHALL BE GATHERED FOR THE WINEPRESS, AND LIKE NEW WINE I SHALL BE KEPT IN ETERNAL VESSELS."

AND IN WINTER, WHEN YOU DRAW THE WINE, LET THERE BE IN YOUR HEART A SONG FOR EACH CUP;

AND LET THERE BE IN THE SONG A REMEMBRANCE FOR THE AUTUMN DAYS, AND FOR THE VINEYARD, AND FOR THE WINEPRESS.

THEN SAID A RICH MAN, SPEAK TO US OF GIVING.

AND HE ANSWERED:

YOU GIVE BUT LITTLE WHEN YOU GIVE OF YOUR POSSESSIONS.

IT IS WHEN YOU GIVE OF YOURSELF THAT YOU TRULY GIVE.

FOR WHAT ARE YOUR POSSESSIONS BUT THINGS YOU KEEP AND GUARD FOR FEAR YOU MAY NEED THEM TOMORROW?

AND TOMORROW, WHAT SHALL TOMORROW BRING TO THE OVERPRUDENT DOG BURYING BONES IN THE TRACKLESS SAND AS HE FOLLOWS THE PILGRIMS TO THE HOLY CITY?

AND WHAT IS FEAR OF NEED BUT NEED ITSELF?

IS NOT DREAD OF THIRST WHEN YOUR WELL IS FULL, THE THIRST THAT IS UNQUENCHABLE?

THERE ARE THOSE WHO GIVE LITTLE OF THE MUCH WHICH THEY HAVE--AND THEY GIVE IT FOR RECOGNITION AND THEIR HIDDEN DESIRE MAKES THEIR GIFTS UNWHOLESOME.

AND THERE ARE THOSE WHO HAVE LITTLE AND GIVE IT ALL.

THESE ARE THE BELIEVERS IN LIFE AND THE BOUNTY OF LIFE, AND THEIR COFFER IS NEVER EMPTY.

THERE ARE THOSE WHO GIVE WITH JOY, AND THAT JOY IS THEIR REWARD.

AND THERE ARE THOSE WHO GIVE WITH PAIN, AND THAT PAIN IS THEIR BAPTISM.

AND THERE ARE THOSE WHO GIVE AND KNOW NOT PAIN IN GIVING, NOR DO THEY SEEK JOY, NOR GIVE WITH MINDFULNESS OF VIRTUE; THEY GIVE AS IN YONDER VALLEY THE MYRTLE BREATHES ITS FRAGRANCE INTO SPACE.

THROUGH THE HANDS OF SUCH AS THESE GOD SPEAKS, AND FROM BEHIND THEIR EYES HE SMILES UPON THE EARTH.

IT IS WELL TO GIVE WHEN ASKED, BUT IT IS BETTER TO GIVE UNASKED, THROUGH UNDERSTANDING;

AND TO THE OPEN-HANDED THE SEARCH FOR ONE WHO SHALL RECEIVE IS JOY GREATER THAN GIVING.

AND IS THERE AUGHT YOU WOULD WITHHOLD?

ALL YOU HAVE SHALL SOME DAY BE GIVEN;

THEREFORE GIVE NOW, THAT THE SEASON OF GIVING MAY BE YOURS AND NOT YOUR INHERITORS'.

YOU OFTEN SAY, "I WOULD GIVE, BUT ONLY TO THE DESERVING."

THE TREES IN YOUR ORCHARD SAY NOT SO, NOR THE FLOCKS IN YOUR PASTURE.

THEY GIVE THAT THEY MAY LIVE, FOR TO WITHHOLD IS TO PERISH.

SURELY HE WHO IS WORTHY TO RECEIVE HIS DAYS AND HIS NIGHTS IS WORTHY OF ALL ELSE FROM YOU.

AND HE WHO HAS DESERVED TO DRINK FROM THE OCEAN OF LIFE DESERVES TO FILL HIS CUP FROM YOUR LITTLE STREAM.

AND WHAT DESERT GREATER SHALL THERE BE, THAN THAT WHICH LIES IN THE COURAGE AND THE CONFIDENCE, NAY THE CHARITY, OF RECEIVING?

AND WHO ARE YOU THAT MEN SHOULD REND THEIR BOSOM AND UNVEIL THEIR PRIDE, THAT YOU MAY SEE THEIR WORTH NAKED AND THEIR PRIDE UNABASHED?

SEE FIRST THAT YOU YOURSELF DESERVE TO BE A GIVER, AND AN INSTRUMENT OF GIVING.

FOR IN TRUTH IT IS LIFE THAT GIVES UNTO LIFE-- WHILE YOU, WHO DEEM YOURSELF A GIVER, ARE BUT A WITNESS.

AND YOU RECEIVERS--AND YOU ARE ALL RECEIVERS-- ASSUME NO WEIGHT OF GRATITUDE, LEST YOU LAY A YOKE UPON YOURSELF AND UPON HIM WHO GIVES.

RATHER RISE TOGETHER WITH THE GIVER ON HIS GIFTS AS ON WINGS;

FOR TO BE OVERMINDFUL OF YOUR DEBT IS TO DOUBT HIS GENEROSITY WHO HAS THE FREE-HEARTED EARTH FOR MOTHER, AND GOD FOR FATHER.

AND A WOMAN WHO HELD A BABE AGAINST HER BOSOM SAID,
SPEAK TO US OF CHILDREN.

AND HE SAID:

YOUR CHILDREN ARE NOT YOUR CHILDREN.

THEY ARE THE SONS AND DAUGHTERS OF LIFE'S LONGING FOR ITSELF.
THEY COME THROUGH YOU BUT NOT FROM YOU,
AND THOUGH THEY ARE WITH YOU YET THEY BELONG NOT TO YOU.

YOU MAY GIVE THEM YOUR LOVE BUT NOT YOUR THOUGHTS,
FOR THEY HAVE THEIR OWN THOUGHTS.

YOU MAY HOUSE THEIR BODIES BUT NOT THEIR SOULS,
FOR THEIR SOULS DWELL IN THE HOUSE OF TOMORROW, WHICH YOU CANNOT VISIT, NOT EVEN IN YOUR DREAMS.
YOU MAY STRIVE TO BE LIKE THEM, BUT SEEK NOT TO MAKE THEM LIKE YOU.
FOR LIFE GOES NOT BACKWARD NOR TARRIES WITH YESTERDAY.

YOU ARE THE BOWS FROM WHICH YOUR CHILDREN AS LIVING ARROWS ARE SENT FORTH.
THE ARCHER SEES THE MARK UPON THE PATH OF THE INFINITE, AND HE BENDS YOU WITH HIS MIGHT THAT HIS ARROWS MAY GO SWIFT AND FAR.

LET YOUR BENDING IN THE ARCHER'S HAND BE FOR GLADNESS;
FOR EVEN AS HE LOVES THE ARROW THAT FLIES, SO HE LOVES ALSO THE BOW THAT IS STABLE.

THEN SAID A TEACHER, SPEAK TO US OF TEACHING.

AND HE SAID:

NO MAN CAN REVEAL TO YOU AUGHT BUT THAT WHICH ALREADY LIES HALF ASLEEP IN THE DAWNING OF YOUR KNOWLEDGE.

THE TEACHER WHO WALKS IN THE SHADOW OF THE TEMPLE, AMONG HIS FOLLOWERS, GIVES NOT OF HIS WISDOM BUT RATHER OF HIS FAITH AND HIS LOVINGNESS.

IF HE IS INDEED WISE HE DOES NOT BID YOU ENTER THE HOUSE OF HIS WISDOM, BUT RATHER LEADS YOU TO THE THRESHOLD OF YOUR OWN MIND.

THE ASTRONOMER MAY SPEAK TO YOU OF HIS UNDERSTANDING OF SPACE, BUT HE CANNOT GIVE YOU HIS UNDERSTANDING.

THE MUSICIAN MAY SING TO YOU OF THE RHYTHM WHICH IS IN ALL SPACE, BUT HE CANNOT GIVE YOU THE EAR WHICH ARRESTS THE RHYTHM NOR THE VOICE THAT ECHOES IT.

AND HE WHO IS VERSED IN THE SCIENCE OF NUMBERS CAN TELL OF THE REGIONS OF WEIGHT AND MEASURE, BUT HE CANNOT CONDUCT YOU THITHER.

FOR THE VISION OF ONE MAN LENDS NOT ITS WINGS TO ANOTHER MAN.

AND EVEN AS EACH ONE OF YOU STANDS ALONE IN GOD'S KNOWLEDGE, SO MUST EACH ONE OF YOU BE ALONE IN HIS KNOWLEDGE OF GOD AND IN HIS UNDERSTANDING OF THE EARTH.

AND A MERCHANT SAID,
SPEAK TO US OF BUYING AND SELLING.

AND HE ANSWERED AND SAID:

TO YOU THE EARTH YIELDS HER FRUIT, AND YOU SHALL NOT WANT IF YOU BUT KNOW HOW TO FILL YOUR HANDS.

IT IS IN EXCHANGING THE GIFTS OF THE EARTH THAT YOU SHALL FIND ABUNDANCE AND BE SATISFIED.

YET UNLESS THE EXCHANGE BE IN LOVE AND KINDLY JUSTICE IT WILL BUT LEAD SOME TO GREED AND OTHERS TO HUNGER.

WHEN IN THE MARKETPLACE YOU TOILERS OF THE SEA AND FIELDS AND VINEYARDS MEET THE WEAVERS AND THE POTTERS AND THE GATHERERS OF SPICES--

INVOKE THEN THE MASTER SPIRIT OF THE EARTH, TO COME INTO YOUR MIDST AND SANCTIFY THE SCALES AND THE RECKONING THAT WEIGHS VALUE AGAINST VALUE.

AND SUFFER NOT THE BARREN-HANDED TO TAKE PART IN YOUR TRANSACTIONS, WHO WOULD SELL THEIR WORDS FOR YOUR LABOUR.
TO SUCH MEN YOU SHOULD SAY:

"COME WITH US TO THE FIELD, OR GO WITH OUR BROTHERS TO THE SEA AND CAST YOUR NET;
FOR THE LAND AND THE SEA SHALL BE BOUNTIFUL TO YOU EVEN AS TO US."

AND IF THERE COME THE SINGERS AND THE DANCERS AND THE FLUTE PLAYERS-- BUY OF THEIR GIFTS ALSO.

FOR THEY TOO ARE GATHERERS OF FRUIT AND FRANKINCENSE, AND THAT WHICH THEY BRING, THOUGH FASHIONED OF DREAMS, IS RAIMENT AND FOOD FOR YOUR SOUL.

AND BEFORE YOU LEAVE THE MARKETPLACE, SEE THAT NO ONE HAS GONE HIS WAY WITH EMPTY HANDS.

FOR THE MASTER SPIRIT OF THE EARTH SHALL NOT SLEEP PEACEFULLY UPON THE WIND TILL THE NEEDS OF THE LEAST OF YOU ARE SATISFIED.

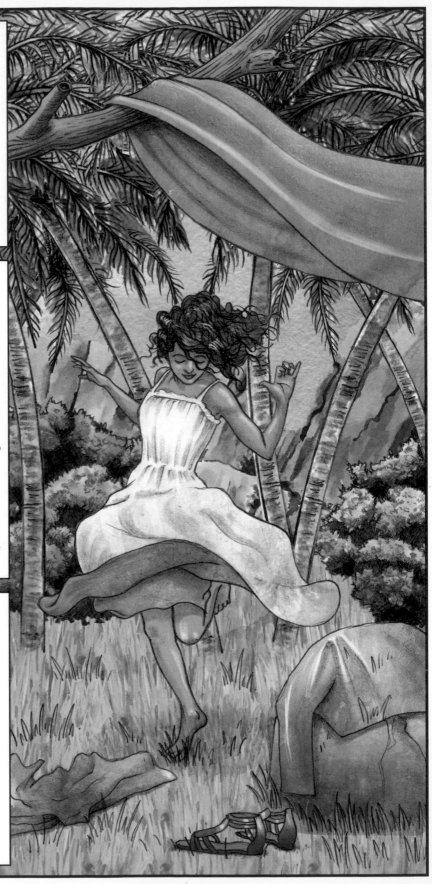

AND THE WEAVER SAID,
SPEAK TO US OF CLOTHES.

AND HE ANSWERED:

YOUR CLOTHES CONCEAL
MUCH OF YOUR BEAUTY,
YET THEY HIDE NOT THE
UNBEAUTIFUL.

AND THOUGH YOU SEEK IN
GARMENTS THE FREEDOM
OF PRIVACY YOU MAY FIND
IN THEM A HARNESS AND A
CHAIN.

WOULD THAT YOU COULD
MEET THE SUN AND THE
WIND WITH MORE OF YOUR
SKIN AND LESS OF YOUR
RAIMENT.

FOR THE BREATH OF LIFE
IS IN THE SUNLIGHT AND
THE HAND OF LIFE IS IN THE
WIND.

SOME OF YOU SAY,
"IT IS THE NORTH WIND WHO
HAS WOVEN THE CLOTHES
WE WEAR."

AND I SAY, AY, IT WAS THE
NORTH WIND,
BUT SHAME WAS HIS LOOM,
AND THE SOFTENING OF THE
SINEWS WAS HIS THREAD.

AND WHEN HIS WORK WAS
DONE HE LAUGHED IN THE
FOREST. FORGET NOT THAT
MODESTY IS FOR A SHIELD
AGAINST THE EYE OF THE
UNCLEAN.

AND WHEN THE UNCLEAN
SHALL BE NO MORE, WHAT
WERE MODESTY BUT A
FETTER AND A FOULING OF
THE MIND?

AND FORGET NOT THAT THE
EARTH DELIGHTS TO FEEL
YOUR BARE FEET AND THE
WINDS LONG TO PLAY WITH
YOUR HAIR.

THEN A MASON CAME FORTH
AND SAID,
SPEAK TO US OF HOUSES.

AND HE ANSWERED AND SAID:

BUILD OF YOUR IMAGININGS A
BOWER IN THE WILDERNESS
ERE YOU BUILD A HOUSE
WITHIN THE CITY WALLS.

FOR EVEN AS YOU HAVE
HOMECOMINGS IN YOUR
TWILIGHT, SO HAS THE
WANDERER IN YOU, THE EVER
DISTANT AND ALONE.

YOUR HOUSE IS YOUR LARGER
BODY.

IT GROWS IN THE SUN AND
SLEEPS IN THE STILLNESS
OF THE NIGHT; AND IT IS
NOT DREAMLESS. DOES NOT
YOUR HOUSE DREAM? AND
DREAMING, LEAVE THE CITY
FOR GROVE OR HILLTOP?

WOULD THAT I COULD GATHER
YOUR HOUSES INTO MY HAND,
AND LIKE A SOWER SCATTER
THEM IN FOREST AND
MEADOW.

WOULD THE VALLEYS WERE
YOUR STREETS, AND THE
GREEN PATHS YOUR ALLEYS,
THAT YOU MIGHT SEEK
ONE ANOTHER THROUGH
VINEYARDS, AND COME WITH
THE FRAGRANCE OF THE
EARTH IN YOUR GARMENTS.

BUT THESE THINGS ARE NOT
YET TO BE.

IN THEIR FEAR YOUR
FOREFATHERS GATHERED YOU
TOO NEAR TOGETHER. AND
THAT FEAR SHALL ENDURE
A LITTLE LONGER. A LITTLE
LONGER SHALL YOUR CITY
WALLS SEPARATE YOUR
HEARTHS FROM YOUR FIELDS.

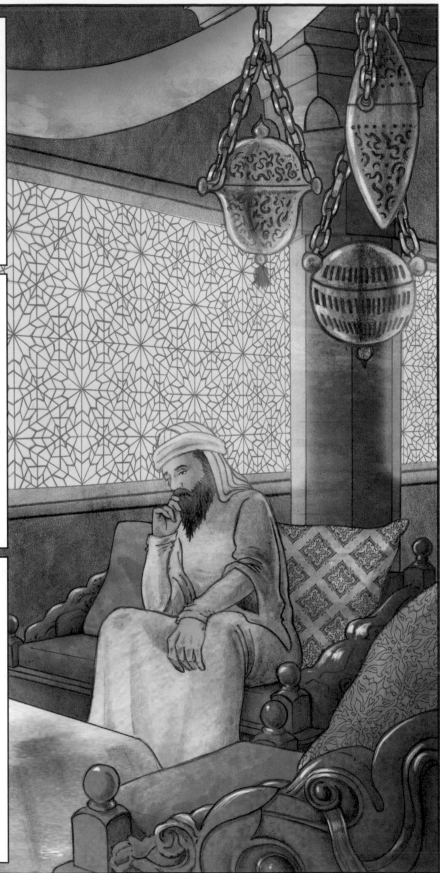

AND TELL ME, PEOPLE OF ORPHALESE, WHAT HAVE YOU IN THESE HOUSES? AND WHAT IS IT YOU GUARD WITH FASTENED DOORS?

HAVE YOU PEACE, THE QUIET URGE THAT REVEALS YOUR POWER?

HAVE YOU REMEMBRANCES, THE GLIMMERING ARCHES THAT SPAN THE SUMMITS OF THE MIND?

HAVE YOU BEAUTY, THAT LEADS THE HEART FROM THINGS FASHIONED OF WOOD AND STONE TO THE HOLY MOUNTAIN?

TELL ME, HAVE YOU THESE IN YOUR HOUSES?

OR HAVE YOU ONLY COMFORT, AND THE LUST FOR COMFORT, THAT STEALTHY THING THAT ENTERS THE HOUSE A GUEST, AND THEN BECOMES A HOST, AND THEN A MASTER?

AY, AND IT BECOMES A TAMER, AND WITH HOOK AND SCOURGE MAKES PUPPETS OF YOUR LARGER DESIRES.

THOUGH ITS HANDS ARE SILKEN, ITS HEART IS OF IRON.

IT LULLS YOU TO SLEEP ONLY TO STAND BY YOUR BED AND JEER AT THE DIGNITY OF THE FLESH.

IT MAKES MOCK OF YOUR SOUND SENSES, AND LAYS THEM IN THISTLEDOWN LIKE FRAGILE VESSELS.

VERILY THE LUST FOR COMFORT MURDERS THE PASSION OF THE SOUL, AND THEN WALKS GRINNING IN THE FUNERAL.

BUT YOU, CHILDREN OF SPACE, YOU RESTLESS IN REST, YOU SHALL NOT BE TRAPPED NOR TAMED.

YOUR HOUSE SHALL BE NOT AN ANCHOR BUT A MAST.

IT SHALL NOT BE A GLISTENING FILM THAT COVERS A WOUND, BUT AN EYELID THAT GUARDS THE EYE.

YOU SHALL NOT FOLD YOUR WINGS THAT YOU MAY PASS THROUGH DOORS, NOR BEND YOUR HEADS THAT THEY STRIKE NOT AGAINST A CEILING, NOR FEAR TO BREATHE LEST WALLS SHOULD CRACK AND FALL DOWN.

YOU SHALL NOT DWELL IN TOMBS MADE BY THE DEAD FOR THE LIVING.

AND THOUGH OF MAGNIFICENCE AND SPLENDOUR, YOUR HOUSE SHALL NOT HOLD YOUR SECRET NOR SHELTER YOUR LONGING.

FOR THAT WHICH IS BOUNDLESS IN YOU ABIDES IN THE MANSION OF THE SKY, WHOSE DOOR IS THE MORNING MIST, AND WHOSE WINDOWS ARE THE SONGS AND THE SILENCES OF NIGHT.

AND A WOMAN SPOKE, SAYING, TELL US OF PAIN.

AND HE SAID:

YOUR PAIN IS THE BREAKING OF THE SHELL THAT ENCLOSES YOUR UNDERSTANDING.

EVEN AS THE STONE OF THE FRUIT MUST BREAK, THAT ITS HEART MAY STAND IN THE SUN, SO MUST YOU KNOW PAIN.

AND COULD YOU KEEP YOUR HEART IN WONDER AT THE DAILY MIRACLES OF YOUR LIFE, YOUR PAIN WOULD NOT SEEM LESS WONDROUS THAN YOUR JOY;
AND YOU WOULD ACCEPT THE SEASONS OF YOUR HEART, EVEN AS YOU HAVE ALWAYS ACCEPTED THE SEASONS THAT PASS OVER YOUR FIELDS.

AND YOU WOULD WATCH WITH SERENITY THROUGH THE WINTERS OF YOUR GRIEF.
MUCH OF YOUR PAIN IS SELF-CHOSEN.

IT IS THE BITTER POTION BY WHICH THE PHYSICIAN WITHIN YOU HEALS YOUR SICK SELF.

THEREFORE TRUST THE PHYSICIAN, AND DRINK HIS REMEDY IN SILENCE AND TRANQUILLITY:
FOR HIS HAND, THOUGH HEAVY AND HARD, IS GUIDED BY THE TENDER HAND OF THE UNSEEN,
AND THE CUP HE BRINGS, THOUGH IT BURN YOUR LIPS, HAS BEEN FASHIONED OF THE CLAY WHICH THE POTTER HAS MOISTENED WITH HIS OWN SACRED TEARS.

AND THE PRIESTESS SPOKE AGAIN AND SAID: SPEAK TO US OF REASON AND PASSION.

AND HE ANSWERED, SAYING:

YOUR SOUL IS OFTENTIMES A BATTLEFIELD, UPON WHICH YOUR REASON AND YOUR JUDGMENT WAGE WAR AGAINST YOUR PASSION AND YOUR APPETITE.

WOULD THAT I COULD BE THE PEACEMAKER IN YOUR SOUL, THAT I MIGHT TURN THE DISCORD AND THE RIVALRY OF YOUR ELEMENTS INTO ONENESS AND MELODY.

BUT HOW SHALL I, UNLESS YOU YOURSELVES BE ALSO THE PEACEMAKERS, NAY, THE LOVERS OF ALL YOUR ELEMENTS?

YOUR REASON AND YOUR PASSION ARE THE RUDDER AND THE SAILS OF YOUR SEAFARING SOUL.

IF EITHER YOUR SAILS OR YOUR RUDDER BE BROKEN, YOU CAN BUT TOSS AND DRIFT, OR ELSE BE HELD AT A STANDSTILL IN MID-SEAS.

FOR REASON, RULING ALONE, IS A FORCE CONFINING; AND PASSION, UNATTENDED, IS A FLAME THAT BURNS TO ITS OWN DESTRUCTION.

THEREFORE LET YOUR SOUL EXALT YOUR REASON TO THE HEIGHT OF PASSION, THAT IT MAY SING;
AND LET IT DIRECT YOUR PASSION WITH REASON, THAT YOUR PASSION MAY LIVE THROUGH ITS OWN DAILY RESURRECTION, AND LIKE THE PHOENIX RISE ABOVE ITS OWN ASHES.

I WOULD HAVE YOU CONSIDER YOUR JUDGMENT AND YOUR APPETITE EVEN AS YOU WOULD TWO LOVED GUESTS IN YOUR HOUSE.

SURELY YOU WOULD NOT HONOUR ONE GUEST ABOVE THE OTHER; FOR HE WHO IS MORE MINDFUL OF ONE LOSES THE LOVE AND THE FAITH OF BOTH.

AMONG THE HILLS, WHEN YOU SIT IN THE COOL SHADE OF THE WHITE POPLARS, SHARING THE PEACE AND SERENITY OF DISTANT FIELDS AND MEADOWS--THEN LET YOUR HEART SAY IN SILENCE, "GOD RESTS IN REASON."

AND WHEN THE STORM COMES, AND THE MIGHTY WIND SHAKES THE FOREST, AND THUNDER AND LIGHTNING PROCLAIM THE MAJESTY OF THE SKY--THEN LET YOUR HEART SAY IN AWE, "GOD MOVES IN PASSION."

AND SINCE YOU ARE A BREATH IN GOD'S SPHERE, AND A LEAF IN GOD'S FOREST, YOU TOO SHOULD REST IN REASON AND MOVE IN PASSION.

THEN A WOMAN SAID, SPEAK TO US OF JOY AND SORROW.

AND HE ANSWERED:

YOUR JOY IS YOUR SORROW UNMASKED.

AND THE SELFSAME WELL FROM WHICH YOUR LAUGHTER RISES WAS OFTENTIMES FILLED WITH YOUR TEARS.

AND HOW ELSE CAN IT BE?

THE DEEPER THAT SORROW CARVES INTO YOUR BEING, THE MORE JOY YOU CAN CONTAIN.

IS NOT THE CUP THAT HOLDS YOUR WINE THE VERY CUP THAT WAS BURNED IN THE POTTER'S OVEN?

AND IS NOT THE LUTE THAT SOOTHES YOUR SPIRIT THE VERY WOOD THAT WAS HOLLOWED WITH KNIVES?

WHEN YOU ARE JOYOUS, LOOK DEEP INTO YOUR HEART AND YOU SHALL FIND IT IS ONLY THAT WHICH HAS GIVEN YOU SORROW THAT IS GIVING YOU JOY.

WHEN YOU ARE SORROWFUL LOOK AGAIN IN YOUR HEART, AND YOU SHALL SEE THAT IN TRUTH YOU ARE WEEPING FOR THAT WHICH HAS BEEN YOUR DELIGHT.

SOME OF YOU SAY, "JOY IS GREATER THAN SORROW," AND OTHERS SAY, "NAY, SORROW IS THE GREATER."

BUT I SAY UNTO YOU, THEY ARE INSEPARABLE.

TOGETHER THEY COME, AND WHEN ONE SITS ALONE WITH YOU AT YOUR BOARD, REMEMBER THAT THE OTHER IS ASLEEP UPON YOUR BED.

VERILY YOU ARE SUSPENDED LIKE SCALES BETWEEN YOUR SORROW AND YOUR JOY.

ONLY WHEN YOU ARE EMPTY ARE YOU AT STANDSTILL AND BALANCED.

WHEN THE TREASURE-KEEPER LIFTS YOU TO WEIGH HIS GOLD AND HIS SILVER, NEEDS MUST YOUR JOY OR YOUR SORROW RISE OR FALL.

Part 5

THE WEEKS PASS AND THE
DAYS BLUR...

AND AN ORATOR SAID, SPEAK TO US OF FREEDOM.

AND HE ANSWERED:

AT THE CITY GATE AND BY YOUR FIRESIDE I HAVE SEEN YOU PROSTRATE YOURSELF AND WORSHIP YOUR OWN FREEDOM, EVEN AS SLAVES HUMBLE THEMSELVES BEFORE A TYRANT AND PRAISE HIM THOUGH HE SLAYS THEM.

AY, IN THE GROVE OF THE TEMPLE AND IN THE SHADOW OF THE CITADEL I HAVE SEEN THE FREEST AMONG YOU WEAR THEIR FREEDOM AS A YOKE AND A HANDCUFF.

AND MY HEART BLED WITHIN ME; FOR YOU CAN ONLY BE FREE WHEN EVEN THE DESIRE OF SEEKING FREEDOM BECOMES A HARNESS TO YOU, AND WHEN YOU CEASE TO SPEAK OF FREEDOM AS A GOAL AND A FULFILMENT.

YOU SHALL BE FREE INDEED WHEN YOUR DAYS ARE NOT WITHOUT A CARE NOR YOUR NIGHTS WITHOUT A WANT AND A GRIEF,

BUT RATHER WHEN THESE THINGS GIRDLE YOUR LIFE AND YET YOU RISE ABOVE THEM NAKED AND UNBOUND.

AND HOW SHALL YOU RISE BEYOND YOUR DAYS AND NIGHTS UNLESS YOU BREAK THE CHAINS WHICH YOU AT THE DAWN OF YOUR UNDERSTANDING HAVE FASTENED AROUND YOUR NOON HOUR?

IN TRUTH THAT WHICH YOU CALL FREEDOM IS THE STRONGEST OF THESE CHAINS, THOUGH ITS LINKS GLITTER IN THE SUN AND DAZZLE YOUR EYES.

AND WHAT IS IT BUT FRAGMENTS OF YOUR OWN SELF YOU WOULD DISCARD THAT YOU MAY BECOME FREE?

IF IT IS AN UNJUST LAW YOU WOULD ABOLISH, THAT LAW WAS WRITTEN WITH YOUR OWN HAND UPON YOUR OWN FOREHEAD.

YOU CANNOT ERASE IT BY BURNING YOUR LAW BOOKS NOR BY WASHING THE FOREHEADS OF YOUR JUDGES, THOUGH YOU POUR THE SEA UPON THEM.

AND IF IT IS A DESPOT YOU WOULD DETHRONE, SEE FIRST THAT HIS THRONE ERECTED WITHIN YOU IS DESTROYED.

FOR HOW CAN A TYRANT RULE THE FREE AND THE PROUD, BUT FOR A TYRANNY IN THEIR OWN FREEDOM AND A SHAME IN THEIR OWN PRIDE?

AND IF IT IS A CARE YOU WOULD CAST OFF, THAT CARE HAS BEEN CHOSEN BY YOU RATHER THAN IMPOSED UPON YOU.

AND IF IT IS A FEAR YOU WOULD DISPEL, THE SEAT OF THAT FEAR IS IN YOUR HEART AND NOT IN THE HAND OF THE FEARED.

VERILY ALL THINGS MOVE WITHIN YOUR BEING IN CONSTANT HALF EMBRACE, THE DESIRED AND THE DREADED, THE REPUGNANT AND THE CHERISHED, THE PURSUED AND THAT WHICH YOU WOULD ESCAPE.

THESE THINGS MOVE WITHIN YOU AS LIGHTS AND SHADOWS IN PAIRS THAT CLING.

AND WHEN THE SHADOW FADES AND IS NO MORE, THE LIGHT THAT LINGERS BECOMES A SHADOW TO ANOTHER LIGHT.

AND THUS YOUR FREEDOM WHEN IT LOSES ITS FETTERS BECOMES ITSELF THE FETTER OF A GREATER FREEDOM.

THEN A PLOUGHMAN SAID, SPEAK TO US OF WORK.

AND HE ANSWERED, SAYING:

YOU WORK THAT YOU MAY KEEP PACE WITH THE EARTH AND THE SOUL OF THE EARTH.

FOR TO BE IDLE IS TO BECOME A STRANGER UNTO THE SEASONS, AND TO STEP OUT OF LIFE'S PROCESSION THAT MARCHES IN MAJESTY AND PROUD SUBMISSION TOWARDS THE INFINITE.

WHEN YOU WORK YOU ARE A FLUTE THROUGH WHOSE HEART THE WHISPERING OF THE HOURS TURNS TO MUSIC.

WHICH OF YOU WOULD BE A REED, DUMB AND SILENT, WHEN ALL ELSE SINGS TOGETHER IN UNISON?

ALWAYS YOU HAVE BEEN TOLD THAT WORK IS A CURSE AND LABOUR A MISFORTUNE.

BUT I SAY TO YOU THAT WHEN YOU WORK YOU FULFIL A PART OF EARTH'S FURTHEST DREAM, ASSIGNED TO YOU WHEN THAT DREAM WAS BORN,
AND IN KEEPING YOURSELF WITH LABOUR YOU ARE IN TRUTH LOVING LIFE,
AND TO LOVE LIFE THROUGH LABOUR IS TO BE INTIMATE WITH LIFE'S INMOST SECRET.

BUT IF YOU IN YOUR PAIN CALL BIRTH AN AFFLICTION AND THE SUPPORT OF THE FLESH A CURSE WRITTEN UPON YOUR BROW, THEN I ANSWER THAT NAUGHT BUT THE SWEAT OF YOUR BROW SHALL WASH AWAY THAT WHICH IS WRITTEN.

YOU HAVE BEEN TOLD ALSO THAT LIFE IS DARKNESS, AND IN YOUR WEARINESS YOU ECHO WHAT WAS SAID BY THE WEARY.

AND I SAY THAT LIFE IS INDEED DARKNESS SAVE WHEN THERE IS URGE,

AND ALL URGE IS BLIND SAVE WHEN THERE IS KNOWLEDGE.

AND ALL KNOWLEDGE IS VAIN SAVE WHEN THERE IS WORK,

AND ALL WORK IS EMPTY SAVE WHEN THERE IS LOVE;

AND WHEN YOU WORK WITH LOVE YOU BIND YOURSELF TO YOURSELF, AND TO ONE ANOTHER, AND TO GOD.

AND WHAT IS IT TO WORK WITH LOVE?

IT IS TO WEAVE THE CLOTH WITH THREADS DRAWN FROM YOUR HEART, EVEN AS IF YOUR BELOVED WERE TO WEAR THAT CLOTH.

IT IS TO BUILD A HOUSE WITH AFFECTION, EVEN AS IF YOUR BELOVED WERE TO DWELL IN THAT HOUSE.

IT IS TO SOW SEEDS WITH TENDERNESS AND REAP THE HARVEST WITH JOY, EVEN AS IF YOUR BELOVED WERE TO EAT THE FRUIT.

IT IS TO CHARGE ALL THINGS YOU FASHION WITH A BREATH OF YOUR OWN SPIRIT,

AND TO KNOW THAT ALL THE BLESSED DEAD ARE STANDING ABOUT YOU AND WATCHING.

OFTEN HAVE I HEARD YOU SAY, AS IF SPEAKING IN SLEEP,
"HE WHO WORKS IN MARBLE, AND FINDS THE SHAPE OF HIS OWN SOUL IN THE STONE, IS NOBLER THAN HE WHO PLOUGHS THE SOIL. AND HE WHO SEIZES THE RAINBOW TO LAY IT ON A CLOTH IN THE LIKENESS OF MAN, IS MORE THAN HE WHO MAKES THE SANDALS FOR OUR FEET."

BUT I SAY, NOT IN SLEEP, BUT IN THE OVERWAKEFULNESS OF NOONTIDE, THAT THE WIND SPEAKS NOT MORE SWEETLY TO THE GIANT OAKS THAN TO THE LEAST OF ALL THE BLADES OF GRASS;

AND HE ALONE IS GREAT WHO TURNS THE VOICE OF THE WIND INTO A SONG MADE SWEETER BY HIS OWN LOVING.

WORK IS LOVE MADE VISIBLE.

AND IF YOU CANNOT WORK WITH LOVE BUT ONLY WITH DISTASTE, IT IS BETTER THAT YOU SHOULD LEAVE YOUR WORK AND SIT AT THE GATE OF THE TEMPLE AND TAKE ALMS OF THOSE WHO WORK WITH JOY.

FOR IF YOU BAKE BREAD WITH INDIFFERENCE, YOU BAKE A BITTER BREAD THAT FEEDS BUT HALF MAN'S HUNGER.

AND IF YOU GRUDGE THE CRUSHING OF THE GRAPES, YOUR GRUDGE DISTILS A POISON IN THE WINE.
AND IF YOU SING THOUGH AS ANGELS, AND LOVE NOT THE SINGING, YOU MUFFLE MAN'S EARS TO THE VOICES OF THE DAY AND THE VOICES OF THE NIGHT.

Part 6

BACK HOME...

⊰SIGH⊱

"TO BE IDLE IS TO BECOME A STRANGER TO THE SEASONS, AND TO STEP OUT OF LIFE'S PROCESSION."

MAYBE IT'S TIME TO REJOIN THE PROCESSION.

THEN ONE OF THE JUDGES OF THE CITY STOOD FORTH AND SAID, SPEAK TO US OF CRIME AND PUNISHMENT.

AND HE ANSWERED, SAYING:
IT IS WHEN YOUR SPIRIT GOES WANDERING UPON THE WIND,
THAT YOU, ALONE AND UNGUARDED, COMMIT A WRONG UNTO OTHERS AND THEREFORE UNTO YOURSELF.

AND FOR THAT WRONG COMMITTED MUST YOU KNOCK AND WAIT A WHILE UNHEEDED AT THE GATE OF THE BLESSED.

LIKE THE OCEAN IS YOUR GOD-SELF;
IT REMAINS FOR EVER UNDEFILED.

AND LIKE THE ETHER IT LIFTS BUT THE WINGED.

EVEN LIKE THE SUN IS YOUR GOD-SELF;
IT KNOWS NOT THE WAYS OF THE MOLE NOR SEEKS IT THE HOLES OF THE SERPENT.
BUT YOUR GOD-SELF DWELLS NOT ALONE IN YOUR BEING.

MUCH IN YOU IS STILL MAN, AND MUCH IN YOU IS NOT YET MAN,
BUT A SHAPELESS PYGMY THAT WALKS ASLEEP IN THE MIST SEARCHING FOR ITS OWN AWAKENING.

AND OF THE MAN IN YOU WOULD I NOW SPEAK.

FOR IT IS HE AND NOT YOUR GOD-SELF NOR THE PYGMY IN THE MIST THAT KNOWS CRIME AND THE PUNISHMENT OF CRIME.

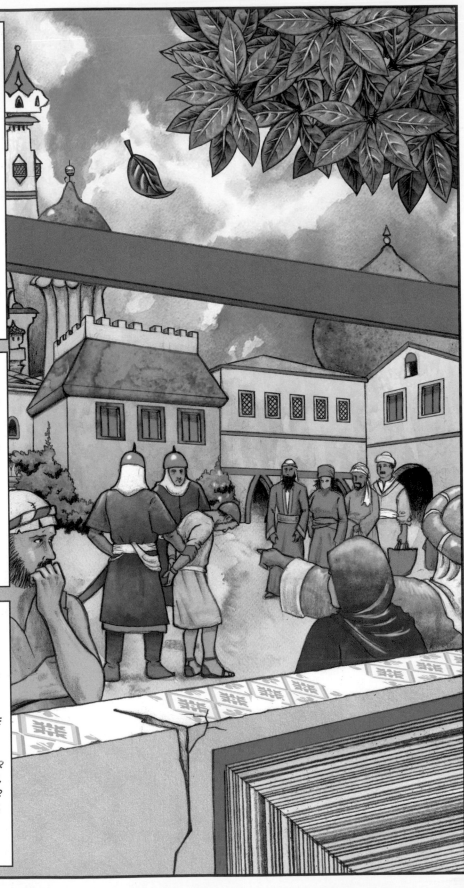

OFTENTIMES HAVE I HEARD YOU SPEAK OF ONE WHO COMMITS A WRONG AS THOUGH HE WERE NOT ONE OF YOU, BUT A STRANGER UNTO YOU AND AN INTRUDER UPON YOUR WORLD.

BUT I SAY THAT EVEN AS THE HOLY AND THE RIGHTEOUS CANNOT RISE BEYOND THE HIGHEST WHICH IS IN EACH ONE OF YOU, SO THE WICKED AND THE WEAK CANNOT FALL LOWER THAN THE LOWEST WHICH IS IN YOU ALSO.

AND AS A SINGLE LEAF TURNS NOT YELLOW BUT WITH THE SILENT KNOWLEDGE OF THE WHOLE TREE, SO THE WRONG-DOER CANNOT DO WRONG WITHOUT THE HIDDEN WILL OF YOU ALL.

LIKE A PROCESSION YOU WALK TOGETHER TOWARDS YOUR GOD-SELF.

YOU ARE THE WAY AND THE WAYFARERS.

AND WHEN ONE OF YOU FALLS DOWN HE FALLS FOR THOSE BEHIND HIM, A CAUTION AGAINST THE STUMBLING STONE.

AY, AND HE FALLS FOR THOSE AHEAD OF HIM, WHO, THOUGH FASTER AND SURER OF FOOT, YET REMOVED NOT THE STUMBLING STONE.

AND THIS ALSO,
THOUGH THE WORD
LIE HEAVY UPON YOUR
HEARTS:

THE MURDERED IS NOT
UNACCOUNTABLE FOR
HIS OWN MURDER,
AND THE ROBBED IS
NOT BLAMELESS IN
BEING ROBBED.

THE RIGHTEOUS IS
NOT INNOCENT OF
THE DEEDS OF THE
WICKED,
AND THE WHITE-
HANDED IS NOT CLEAN
IN THE DOINGS OF THE
FELON.

YEA, THE GUILTY
IS OFTENTIMES
THE VICTIM OF THE
INJURED.
AND STILL MORE
OFTEN THE
CONDEMNED IS THE
BURDEN BEARER FOR
THE GUILTLESS AND
UNBLAMED.

YOU CANNOT
SEPARATE THE JUST
FROM THE UNJUST
AND THE GOOD FROM
THE WICKED;

FOR THEY STAND
TOGETHER BEFORE
THE FACE OF THE SUN
EVEN AS THE BLACK
THREAD AND THE
WHITE ARE WOVEN
TOGETHER.

AND WHEN THE BLACK
THREAD BREAKS, THE
WEAVER SHALL LOOK
INTO THE WHOLE
CLOTH, AND HE SHALL
EXAMINE THE LOOM
ALSO.

IF ANY OF YOU WOULD BRING TO JUDGMENT THE UNFAITHFUL WIFE, LET HIM ALSO WEIGH THE HEART OF HER HUSBAND IN SCALES, AND MEASURE HIS SOUL WITH MEASUREMENTS.

AND LET HIM WHO WOULD LASH THE OFFENDER LOOK UNTO THE SPIRIT OF THE OFFENDED.

AND IF ANY OF YOU WOULD PUNISH IN THE NAME OF RIGHTEOUSNESS AND LAY THE AXE UNTO THE EVIL TREE, LET HIM SEE TO ITS ROOTS;

AND VERILY HE WILL FIND THE ROOTS OF THE GOOD AND THE BAD, THE FRUITFUL AND THE FRUITLESS, ALL ENTWINED TOGETHER IN THE SILENT HEART OF THE EARTH.

AND YOU JUDGES WHO WOULD BE JUST, WHAT JUDGMENT PRONOUNCE YOU UPON HIM WHO THOUGH HONEST IN THE FLESH YET IS A THIEF IN SPIRIT?

WHAT PENALTY LAY YOU UPON HIM WHO SLAYS IN THE FLESH YET IS HIMSELF SLAIN IN THE SPIRIT?

AND HOW PROSECUTE YOU HIM WHO IN ACTION IS A DECEIVER AND AN OPPRESSOR, YET WHO ALSO IS AGGRIEVED AND OUTRAGED?

AND HOW SHALL YOU PUNISH THOSE WHOSE REMORSE IS ALREADY GREATER THAN THEIR MISDEEDS?

IS NOT REMORSE THE JUSTICE WHICH IS ADMINISTERED BY THAT VERY LAW WHICH YOU WOULD FAIN SERVE?

YET YOU CANNOT LAY REMORSE UPON THE INNOCENT NOR LIFT IT FROM THE HEART OF THE GUILTY.

UNBIDDEN SHALL IT CALL IN THE NIGHT, THAT MEN MAY WAKE AND GAZE UPON THEMSELVES.

AND YOU WHO WOULD UNDERSTAND JUSTICE, HOW SHALL YOU UNLESS YOU LOOK UPON ALL DEEDS IN THE FULLNESS OF LIGHT?

ONLY THEN SHALL YOU KNOW THAT THE ERECT AND THE FALLEN ARE BUT ONE MAN STANDING IN TWILIGHT BETWEEN THE NIGHT OF HIS PYGMY-SELF AND THE DAY OF HIS GOD-SELF, AND THAT THE CORNER-STONE OF THE TEMPLE IS NOT HIGHER THAN THE LOWEST STONE IN ITS FOUNDATION.

THEN A LAWYER SAID, BUT WHAT OF OUR LAWS, MASTER?

AND HE ANSWERED:
YOU DELIGHT IN LAYING DOWN LAWS,
YET YOU DELIGHT MORE IN BREAKING THEM.

LIKE CHILDREN PLAYING BY THE OCEAN WHO BUILD SAND-TOWERS WITH CONSTANCY AND THEN DESTROY THEM WITH LAUGHTER.

BUT WHILE YOU BUILD YOUR SAND-TOWERS THE OCEAN BRINGS MORE SAND TO THE SHORE,
AND WHEN YOU DESTROY THEM THE OCEAN LAUGHS WITH YOU.

VERILY THE OCEAN LAUGHS ALWAYS WITH THE INNOCENT.

BUT WHAT OF THOSE TO WHOM LIFE IS NOT AN OCEAN, AND MAN-MADE LAWS ARE NOT SAND-TOWERS,
BUT TO WHOM LIFE IS A ROCK, AND THE LAW A CHISEL WITH WHICH THEY WOULD CARVE IT IN THEIR OWN LIKENESS?
WHAT OF THE CRIPPLE WHO HATES DANCERS?

WHAT OF THE OX WHO LOVES HIS YOKE AND DEEMS THE ELK AND DEER OF THE FOREST STRAY AND VAGRANT THINGS?

WHAT OF THE OLD SERPENT WHO CANNOT SHED HIS SKIN, AND CALLS ALL OTHERS NAKED AND SHAMELESS?

AND OF HIM WHO COMES EARLY TO THE WEDDING-FEAST, AND WHEN OVERFED AND TIRED GOES HIS WAY SAYING THAT ALL FEASTS ARE VIOLATION AND ALL FEASTERS LAWBREAKERS?

WHAT SHALL I SAY OF THESE SAVE THAT THEY TOO STAND IN THE SUNLIGHT, BUT WITH THEIR BACKS TO THE SUN?

THEY SEE ONLY THEIR SHADOWS, AND THEIR SHADOWS ARE THEIR LAWS.

AND WHAT IS THE SUN TO THEM BUT A CASTER OF SHADOWS?

AND WHAT IS IT TO ACKNOWLEDGE THE LAWS BUT TO STOOP DOWN AND TRACE THEIR SHADOWS UPON THE EARTH?

BUT YOU WHO WALK FACING THE SUN, WHAT IMAGES DRAWN ON THE EARTH CAN HOLD YOU?

YOU WHO TRAVEL WITH THE WIND, WHAT WEATHER-VANE SHALL DIRECT YOUR COURSE?

WHAT MAN'S LAW SHALL BIND YOU IF YOU BREAK YOUR YOKE BUT UPON NO MAN'S PRISON DOOR?

WHAT LAWS SHALL YOU FEAR IF YOU DANCE BUT STUMBLE AGAINST NO MAN'S IRON CHAINS?

AND WHO IS HE THAT SHALL BRING YOU TO JUDGMENT IF YOU TEAR OFF YOUR GARMENT YET LEAVE IT IN NO MAN'S PATH?

PEOPLE OF ORPHALESE, YOU CAN MUFFLE THE DRUM, AND YOU CAN LOOSEN THE STRINGS OF THE LYRE, BUT WHO SHALL COMMAND THE SKYLARK NOT TO SING?

I AM COMPLETELY FINE IN THIS MOMENT, MY LOVE. DON'T WORRY.

THAT'S ALL I SEEM TO DO THESE DAYS.

SO IT WOULD APPEAR.

I FEEL LIKE I'M CRACKING UP.

LISTEN, I APPRECIATE ALL THE CONCERN, BUT YOU NEED TO FOCUS LESS ON ME AND MORE ON YOURSELF.

I KNOW IT'S A HARD SITUATION, BUT I CAN'T BE YOUR REASON FOR LETTING LIFE PASS YOU BY. GO OUT. SEE YOUR FRIENDS. GOD FORBID, FIND SOMEONE SPECIAL.

I'LL TRY.

THAT'S MY ALMITRA.

PAPA, WHERE DID THAT NAME COME FROM? DID IT COME FROM THE PROPHET?

YOU DON'T REMEMBER? WELL, LET ME TELL YOU...

"ON THE DAY THAT YOU WERE BORN, YOU NEVER SHED A TEAR. THE NURSES THOUGHT YOU WERE STRANGE AND WHISPERED ABOUT YOU, SAYING IT WASN'T NATURAL. BUT I WATCHED YOU ALL DAY. I COULDN'T TAKE MY EYES OFF YOU. YOU WERE SO BEAUTIFUL."

"AND ALL DAY LONG YOU JUST LOOKED. JUST LOOKED AROUND YOU, CALM AS ANYTHING. SOAKING UP THE WORLD WITH YOUR EYES. BUT ALMOST AS IF YOU ALREADY KNEW WHAT EVERYTHING WAS. THAT YOU HELD SOME INNER KNOWLEDGE. YOUR MOTHER AND I KNEW THAT DAY THAT WE WOULD CALL YOU ALMITRA. AFTER THE BEAUTIFUL SEERESS FROM ORPHALESE."

WHY DIDN'T YOU EVER TELL ME?

I DID. WE TALKED ABOUT IT ON THE DAY YOUR MOTHER PASSED ON.

OH. I BURIED ALL MY MEMORIES OF THAT DAY.

72

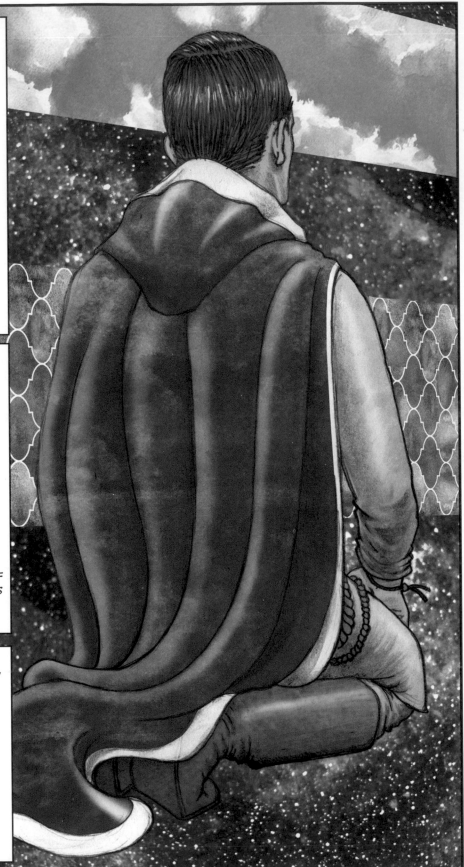

AND A MAN SAID,
SPEAK TO US OF
SELF-KNOWLEDGE.

AND HE ANSWERED,
SAYING:

YOUR HEARTS KNOW
IN SILENCE THE
SECRETS OF THE DAYS
AND THE NIGHTS.

BUT YOUR EARS
THIRST FOR THE
SOUND OF YOUR
HEART'S KNOWLEDGE.

YOU WOULD KNOW IN
WORDS THAT WHICH
YOU HAVE ALWAYS
KNOWN IN THOUGHT.

YOU WOULD TOUCH
WITH YOUR FINGERS
THE NAKED BODY OF
YOUR DREAMS.

AND IT IS WELL YOU
SHOULD.

THE HIDDEN WELL-
SPRING OF YOUR
SOUL MUST NEEDS
RISE AND RUN
MURMURING TO THE
SEA;

AND THE TREASURE OF
YOUR INFINITE DEPTHS
WOULD BE REVEALED
TO YOUR EYES.

BUT LET THERE BE
NO SCALES TO WEIGH
YOUR UNKNOWN
TREASURE;

AND SEEK NOT THE
DEPTHS OF YOUR
KNOWLEDGE WITH
STAFF OR SOUNDING
LINE.

FOR SELF IS A SEA
BOUNDLESS AND
MEASURELESS.

SAY NOT,

"I HAVE FOUND THE TRUTH."

BUT RATHER,

"I HAVE FOUND A TRUTH."

SAY NOT,

"I HAVE FOUND THE PATH OF THE SOUL."

SAY RATHER,

"I HAVE MET THE SOUL WALKING UPON MY PATH."

FOR THE SOUL WALKS UPON ALL PATHS.

THE SOUL WALKS NOT UPON A LINE, NEITHER DOES IT GROW LIKE A REED.

THE SOUL UNFOLDS ITSELF, LIKE A LOTUS OF COUNTLESS PETALS.

AND THEN A SCHOLAR SAID,
SPEAK OF TALKING.

AND HE ANSWERED, SAYING:

YOU TALK WHEN YOU CEASE TO BE AT PEACE WITH YOUR THOUGHTS;

AND WHEN YOU CAN NO LONGER DWELL IN THE SOLITUDE OF YOUR HEART YOU LIVE IN YOUR LIPS, AND SOUND IS A DIVERSION AND A PASTIME.

AND IN MUCH OF YOUR TALKING, THINKING IS HALF MURDERED.

FOR THOUGHT IS A BIRD OF SPACE, THAT IN A CAGE OF WORDS MAY INDEED UNFOLD ITS WINGS BUT CANNOT FLY.

THERE ARE THOSE AMONG YOU WHO SEEK THE TALKATIVE THROUGH FEAR OF BEING ALONE.

THE SILENCE OF ALONENESS REVEALS TO THEIR EYES THEIR NAKED SELVES AND THEY WOULD ESCAPE.

AND THERE ARE THOSE WHO TALK, AND WITHOUT KNOWLEDGE OR FORETHOUGHT REVEAL A TRUTH WHICH THEY THEMSELVES DO NOT UNDERSTAND.

AND THERE ARE THOSE WHO HAVE THE TRUTH WITHIN THEM, BUT THEY TELL IT NOT IN WORDS.

IN THE BOSOM OF SUCH AS THESE THE SPIRIT DWELLS IN RHYTHMIC SILENCE.

WHEN YOU MEET YOUR FRIEND ON THE ROADSIDE OR IN THE MARKETPLACE, LET THE SPIRIT IN YOU MOVE YOUR LIPS AND DIRECT YOUR TONGUE.

LET THE VOICE WITHIN YOUR VOICE SPEAK TO THE EAR OF HIS EAR; FOR HIS SOUL WILL KEEP THE TRUTH OF YOUR HEART AS THE TASTE OF THE WINE IS REMEMBERED WHEN THE COLOUR IS FORGOTTEN AND THE VESSEL IS NO MORE.

AND A YOUTH SAID, SPEAK TO US OF FRIENDSHIP.

AND HE ANSWERED, SAYING:
YOUR FRIEND IS YOUR NEEDS ANSWERED.

HE IS YOUR FIELD WHICH YOU SOW WITH LOVE AND REAP WITH THANKSGIVING.
AND HE IS YOUR BOARD AND YOUR FIRESIDE.

FOR YOU COME TO HIM WITH YOUR HUNGER, AND YOU SEEK HIM FOR PEACE.

WHEN YOUR FRIEND SPEAKS HIS MIND YOU FEAR NOT THE "NAY" IN YOUR OWN MIND, NOR DO YOU WITHHOLD THE "AY."

AND WHEN HE IS SILENT YOUR HEART CEASES NOT TO LISTEN TO HIS HEART; FOR WITHOUT WORDS, IN FRIENDSHIP, ALL THOUGHTS, ALL DESIRES, ALL EXPECTATIONS ARE BORN AND SHARED, WITH JOY THAT IS UNACCLAIMED.

WHEN YOU PART FROM YOUR FRIEND, YOU GRIEVE NOT;

FOR THAT WHICH YOU LOVE MOST IN HIM MAY BE CLEARER IN HIS ABSENCE, AS THE MOUNTAIN TO THE CLIMBER IS CLEARER FROM THE PLAIN.

AND LET THERE BE NO PURPOSE IN FRIENDSHIP SAVE THE DEEPENING OF THE SPIRIT.

FOR LOVE THAT SEEKS AUGHT BUT THE DISCLOSURE OF ITS OWN MYSTERY IS NOT LOVE BUT A NET CAST FORTH: AND ONLY THE UNPROFITABLE IS CAUGHT.

AND LET YOUR BEST BE FOR YOUR FRIEND.

IF HE MUST KNOW THE EBB OF YOUR TIDE, LET HIM KNOW ITS FLOOD ALSO.

FOR WHAT IS YOUR FRIEND THAT YOU SHOULD SEEK HIM WITH HOURS TO KILL?

SEEK HIM ALWAYS WITH HOURS TO LIVE.

FOR IT IS HIS TO FILL YOUR NEED, BUT NOT YOUR EMPTINESS.

AND IN THE SWEETNESS OF FRIENDSHIP LET THERE BE LAUGHTER, AND SHARING OF PLEASURES.

FOR IN THE DEW OF LITTLE THINGS THE HEART FINDS ITS MORNING AND IS REFRESHED.

HOW'S YOUR DAD? I HAVEN'T BEEN IN THERE THIS WEEK.

HE'S OKAY, THANKS. THE SAME. BUT I DID HAVE A WEIRD DREAM ABOUT HIM.

YOU DID?

HE THANKED ME FOR WORRYING ABOUT HIM, BUT SAID I NEED TO STOP USING HIM AS AN EXCUSE FOR AVOIDING LIFE.

WOW. WELL, HE DOES HAVE AN EXCELLENT POINT.

EXCEPT THAT IT WASN'T HIM, WAS IT? IT WAS A DREAM.

"IN SOMNIS VERITAS." IN DREAMS, THERE IS TRUTH!

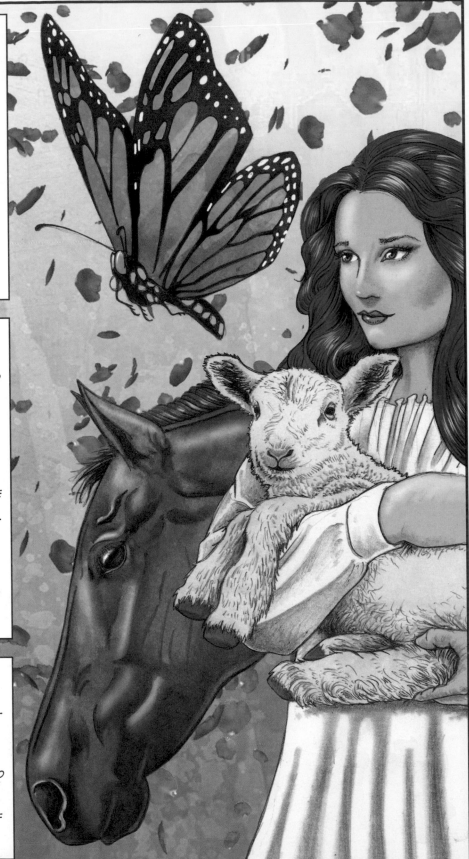

AND A POET SAID,
SPEAK TO US OF
BEAUTY.

AND HE ANSWERED:

WHERE SHALL YOU
SEEK BEAUTY, AND
HOW SHALL YOU
FIND HER UNLESS
SHE HERSELF BE
YOUR WAY AND YOUR
GUIDE?

AND HOW SHALL
YOU SPEAK OF HER
EXCEPT SHE BE THE
WEAVER OF YOUR
SPEECH?

THE AGGRIEVED AND
THE INJURED SAY,
"BEAUTY IS KIND AND
GENTLE.
LIKE A YOUNG
MOTHER HALF-SHY
OF HER OWN GLORY
SHE WALKS AMONG
US."

AND THE PASSIONATE
SAY, "NAY, BEAUTY
IS A THING OF MIGHT
AND DREAD.
LIKE THE TEMPEST
SHE SHAKES THE
EARTH BENEATH US
AND THE SKY ABOVE
US."

THE TIRED AND
THE WEARY SAY,
"BEAUTY IS OF SOFT
WHISPERINGS. SHE
SPEAKS IN OUR
SPIRIT.
HER VOICE YIELDS TO
OUR SILENCES LIKE
A FAINT LIGHT THAT
QUIVERS IN FEAR OF
THE SHADOW."

BUT THE RESTLESS SAY, "WE HAVE HEARD HER SHOUTING AMONG THE MOUNTAINS, AND WITH HER CRIES CAME THE SOUND OF HOOFS, AND THE BEATING OF WINGS AND THE ROARING OF LIONS."

AT NIGHT THE WATCHMEN OF THE CITY SAY, "BEAUTY SHALL RISE WITH THE DAWN FROM THE EAST."

AND AT NOONTIDE THE TOILERS AND THE WAYFARERS SAY, "WE HAVE SEEN HER LEANING OVER THE EARTH FROM THE WINDOWS OF THE SUNSET."

IN WINTER SAY THE SNOW-BOUND, "SHE SHALL COME WITH THE SPRING LEAPING UPON THE HILLS."

AND IN THE SUMMER HEAT THE REAPERS SAY, "WE HAVE SEEN HER DANCING WITH THE AUTUMN LEAVES, AND WE SAW A DRIFT OF SNOW IN HER HAIR."

ALL THESE THINGS HAVE YOU SAID OF BEAUTY,

YET IN TRUTH YOU SPOKE NOT OF HER BUT OF NEEDS UNSATISFIED,

AND BEAUTY IS NOT A NEED BUT AN ECSTASY.

IT IS NOT A MOUTH THIRSTING NOR AN EMPTY HAND STRETCHED FORTH,

BUT RATHER A HEART ENFLAMED AND A SOUL ENCHANTED.

IT IS NOT THE IMAGE YOU WOULD SEE NOR THE SONG YOU WOULD HEAR,

BUT RATHER AN IMAGE YOU SEE THOUGH YOU CLOSE YOUR EYES AND A SONG YOU HEAR THOUGH YOU SHUT YOUR EARS.

IT IS NOT THE SAP WITHIN THE FURROWED BARK, NOR A WING ATTACHED TO A CLAW,

BUT RATHER A GARDEN FOR EVER IN BLOOM AND A FLOCK OF ANGELS FOR EVER IN FLIGHT.

PEOPLE OF ORPHALESE, BEAUTY IS LIFE WHEN LIFE UNVEILS HER HOLY FACE.

BUT YOU ARE LIFE AND YOU ARE THE VEIL.

BEAUTY IS ETERNITY GAZING AT ITSELF IN A MIRROR.

BUT YOU ARE ETERNITY AND YOU ARE THE MIRROR.

AND AN ASTRONOMER SAID,
MASTER, WHAT OF TIME?

AND HE ANSWERED:

YOU WOULD MEASURE TIME
THE MEASURELESS AND THE
IMMEASURABLE.

YOU WOULD ADJUST YOUR
CONDUCT AND EVEN DIRECT
THE COURSE OF YOUR SPIRIT
ACCORDING TO HOURS AND
SEASONS.
OF TIME YOU WOULD MAKE
A STREAM UPON WHOSE BANK
YOU WOULD SIT AND WATCH
ITS FLOWING.

YET THE TIMELESS IN YOU IS
AWARE OF LIFE'S TIMELESSNESS,
AND KNOWS THAT YESTERDAY
IS BUT TODAY'S MEMORY AND
TOMORROW IS TODAY'S DREAM.

AND THAT THAT WHICH SINGS
AND CONTEMPLATES IN YOU
IS STILL DWELLING WITHIN THE
BOUNDS OF THAT FIRST MOMENT
WHICH SCATTERED THE STARS
INTO SPACE.

WHO AMONG YOU DOES NOT
FEEL THAT HIS POWER TO LOVE
IS BOUNDLESS?

AND YET WHO DOES NOT FEEL
THAT VERY LOVE, THOUGH
BOUNDLESS, ENCOMPASSED
WITHIN THE CENTRE OF HIS
BEING, AND MOVING NOT
FROM LOVE THOUGHT TO LOVE
THOUGHT, NOR FROM LOVE
DEEDS TO OTHER LOVE DEEDS?

AND IS NOT TIME EVEN AS LOVE
IS, UNDIVIDED AND PACELESS?

BUT IF IN YOUR THOUGHT YOU
MUST MEASURE TIME INTO
SEASONS, LET EACH SEASON
ENCIRCLE ALL THE OTHER
SEASONS,
AND LET TODAY EMBRACE THE
PAST WITH REMEMBRANCE AND
THE FUTURE WITH LONGING.

THEN A HERMIT, WHO VISITED THE CITY ONCE A YEAR, CAME FORTH AND SAID, SPEAK TO US OF PLEASURE.

AND HE ANSWERED, SAYING:

PLEASURE IS A FREEDOM-SONG, BUT IT IS NOT FREEDOM.

IT IS THE BLOSSOMING OF YOUR DESIRES, BUT IT IS NOT THEIR FRUIT.

IT IS A DEPTH CALLING UNTO A HEIGHT, BUT IT IS NOT THE DEEP NOR THE HIGH.

IT IS THE CAGED TAKING WING, BUT IT IS NOT SPACE ENCOMPASSED.

AY, IN VERY TRUTH, PLEASURE IS A FREEDOM-SONG.

AND I FAIN WOULD HAVE YOU SING IT WITH FULLNESS OF HEART; YET I WOULD NOT HAVE YOU LOSE YOUR HEARTS IN THE SINGING.

SOME OF YOUR YOUTH SEEK PLEASURE AS IF IT WERE ALL, AND THEY ARE JUDGED AND REBUKED. I WOULD NOT JUDGE NOR REBUKE THEM. I WOULD HAVE THEM SEEK.

FOR THEY SHALL FIND PLEASURE, BUT NOT HER ALONE;

SEVEN ARE HER SISTERS, AND THE LEAST OF THEM IS MORE BEAUTIFUL THAN PLEASURE.

HAVE YOU NOT HEARD OF THE MAN WHO WAS DIGGING IN THE EARTH FOR ROOTS AND FOUND A TREASURE?

AND SOME OF YOUR ELDERS REMEMBER PLEASURES WITH REGRET LIKE WRONGS COMMITTED IN DRUNKENNESS.

BUT REGRET IS THE BECLOUDING OF THE MIND AND NOT ITS CHASTISEMENT.

THEY SHOULD REMEMBER THEIR PLEASURES WITH GRATITUDE, AS THEY WOULD THE HARVEST OF A SUMMER.

YET IF IT COMFORTS THEM TO REGRET, LET THEM BE COMFORTED.

AND THERE ARE AMONG YOU THOSE WHO ARE NEITHER YOUNG TO SEEK NOR OLD TO REMEMBER;

AND IN THEIR FEAR OF SEEKING AND REMEMBERING THEY SHUN ALL PLEASURES, LEST THEY NEGLECT THE SPIRIT OR OFFEND AGAINST IT.

BUT EVEN IN THEIR FOREGOING IS THEIR PLEASURE.

AND THUS THEY TOO FIND A TREASURE THOUGH THEY DIG FOR ROOTS WITH QUIVERING HANDS.

BUT TELL ME, WHO IS HE THAT CAN OFFEND THE SPIRIT?

SHALL THE NIGHTINGALE OFFEND THE STILLNESS OF THE NIGHT, OR THE FIREFLY THE STARS?

AND SHALL YOUR FLAME OR YOUR SMOKE BURDEN THE WIND?

THINK YOU THE SPIRIT IS A STILL POOL WHICH YOU CAN TROUBLE WITH A STAFF?

OFTENTIMES IN DENYING YOURSELF PLEASURE YOU DO BUT STORE THE DESIRE IN THE RECESSES OF YOUR BEING.

WHO KNOWS BUT THAT WHICH SEEMS OMITTED TODAY, WAITS FOR TOMORROW?

EVEN YOUR BODY KNOWS ITS HERITAGE AND ITS RIGHTFUL NEED AND WILL NOT BE DECEIVED.

AND YOUR BODY IS THE HARP OF YOUR SOUL,

AND IT IS YOURS TO BRING FORTH SWEET MUSIC FROM IT OR CONFUSED SOUNDS.

AND NOW YOU ASK IN YOUR HEART, "HOW SHALL WE DISTINGUISH THAT WHICH IS GOOD IN PLEASURE FROM THAT WHICH IS NOT GOOD?"

GO TO YOUR FIELDS AND YOUR GARDENS, AND YOU SHALL LEARN THAT IT IS THE PLEASURE OF THE BEE TO GATHER HONEY OF THE FLOWER,

BUT IT IS ALSO THE PLEASURE OF THE FLOWER TO YIELD ITS HONEY TO THE BEE.

FOR TO THE BEE A FLOWER IS A FOUNTAIN OF LIFE,

AND TO THE FLOWER A BEE IS A MESSENGER OF LOVE,

AND TO BOTH, BEE AND FLOWER, THE GIVING AND THE RECEIVING OF PLEASURE IS A NEED AND AN ECSTASY.

PEOPLE OF ORPHALESE, BE IN YOUR PLEASURES LIKE THE FLOWERS AND THE BEES.

93

AND ONE OF THE ELDERS OF THE CITY SAID, SPEAK TO US OF GOOD AND EVIL.

AND HE ANSWERED:

OF THE GOOD IN YOU I CAN SPEAK, BUT NOT OF THE EVIL.

FOR WHAT IS EVIL BUT GOOD TORTURED BY ITS OWN HUNGER AND THIRST?

VERILY WHEN GOOD IS HUNGRY IT SEEKS FOOD EVEN IN DARK CAVES, AND WHEN IT THIRSTS IT DRINKS EVEN OF DEAD WATERS.

YOU ARE GOOD WHEN YOU ARE ONE WITH YOURSELF.

YET WHEN YOU ARE NOT ONE WITH YOURSELF YOU ARE NOT EVIL.

FOR A DIVIDED HOUSE IS NOT A DEN OF THIEVES; IT IS ONLY A DIVIDED HOUSE.

AND A SHIP WITHOUT RUDDER MAY WANDER AIMLESSLY AMONG PERILOUS ISLES YET SINK NOT TO THE BOTTOM.
YOU ARE GOOD WHEN YOU STRIVE TO GIVE OF YOURSELF.

YET YOU ARE NOT EVIL WHEN YOU SEEK GAIN FOR YOURSELF.

FOR WHEN YOU STRIVE FOR GAIN YOU ARE BUT A ROOT THAT CLINGS TO THE EARTH AND SUCKS AT HER BREAST.

SURELY THE FRUIT CANNOT SAY TO THE ROOT, "BE LIKE ME, RIPE AND FULL AND EVER GIVING OF YOUR ABUNDANCE."

FOR TO THE FRUIT GIVING IS A NEED, AS RECEIVING IS A NEED TO THE ROOT.

YOU ARE GOOD WHEN YOU ARE FULLY AWAKE IN YOUR SPEECH,

YET YOU ARE NOT EVIL WHEN YOU SLEEP WHILE YOUR TONGUE STAGGERS WITHOUT PURPOSE.

AND EVEN STUMBLING SPEECH MAY STRENGTHEN A WEAK TONGUE.

YOU ARE GOOD WHEN YOU WALK TO YOUR GOAL FIRMLY AND WITH BOLD STEPS.

YET YOU ARE NOT EVIL WHEN YOU GO THITHER LIMPING.

EVEN THOSE WHO LIMP GO NOT BACKWARD.

BUT YOU WHO ARE STRONG AND SWIFT, SEE THAT YOU DO NOT LIMP BEFORE THE LAME, DEEMING IT KINDNESS.

YOU ARE GOOD IN COUNTLESS WAYS, AND YOU ARE NOT EVIL WHEN YOU ARE NOT GOOD,

YOU ARE ONLY LOITERING AND SLUGGARD.

PITY THAT THE STAGS CANNOT TEACH SWIFTNESS TO THE TURTLES.

IN YOUR LONGING FOR YOUR GIANT SELF LIES YOUR GOODNESS: AND THAT LONGING IS IN ALL OF YOU.

BUT IN SOME OF YOU THAT LONGING IS A TORRENT RUSHING WITH MIGHT TO THE SEA, CARRYING THE SECRETS OF THE HILLSIDES AND THE SONGS OF THE FOREST.

AND IN OTHERS IT IS A FLAT STREAM THAT LOSES ITSELF IN ANGLES AND BENDS AND LINGERS BEFORE IT REACHES THE SHORE.

BUT LET NOT HIM WHO LONGS MUCH SAY TO HIM WHO LONGS LITTLE, "WHEREFORE ARE YOU SLOW AND HALTING?"

FOR THE TRULY GOOD ASK NOT THE NAKED, "WHERE IS YOUR GARMENT?" NOR THE HOUSELESS, "WHAT HAS BEFALLEN YOUR HOUSE?"

THEN A PRIESTESS SAID, SPEAK TO US OF PRAYER.

AND HE ANSWERED, SAYING:

YOU PRAY IN YOUR DISTRESS AND IN YOUR NEED; WOULD THAT YOU MIGHT PRAY ALSO IN THE FULLNESS OF YOUR JOY AND IN YOUR DAYS OF ABUNDANCE.

FOR WHAT IS PRAYER BUT THE EXPANSION OF YOURSELF INTO THE LIVING ETHER?

AND IF IT IS FOR YOUR COMFORT TO POUR YOUR DARKNESS INTO SPACE, IT IS ALSO FOR YOUR DELIGHT TO POUR FORTH THE DAWNING OF YOUR HEART.

AND IF YOU CANNOT BUT WEEP WHEN YOUR SOUL SUMMONS YOU TO PRAYER, SHE SHOULD SPUR YOU AGAIN AND YET AGAIN, THOUGH WEEPING, UNTIL YOU SHALL COME LAUGHING.

WHEN YOU PRAY YOU RISE TO MEET IN THE AIR THOSE WHO ARE PRAYING AT THAT VERY HOUR, AND WHOM SAVE IN PRAYER YOU MAY NOT MEET.

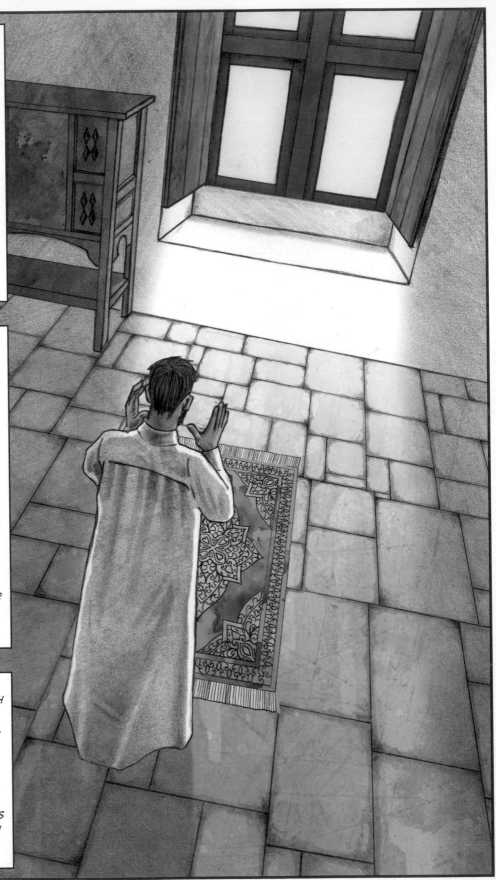

THEREFORE LET
YOUR VISIT TO
THAT TEMPLE
INVISIBLE BE
FOR NAUGHT
BUT ECSTASY
AND SWEET
COMMUNION.

FOR IF YOU
SHOULD ENTER
THE TEMPLE
FOR NO OTHER
PURPOSE THAN
ASKING YOU
SHALL NOT
RECEIVE:

AND IF YOU
SHOULD
ENTER INTO
IT TO HUMBLE
YOURSELF YOU
SHALL NOT BE
LIFTED:

OR EVEN IF YOU
SHOULD ENTER
INTO IT TO BEG
FOR THE GOOD
OF OTHERS YOU
SHALL NOT BE
HEARD.

IT IS ENOUGH
THAT YOU ENTER
THE TEMPLE
INVISIBLE.

I CANNOT TEACH
YOU HOW TO
PRAY IN WORDS.

GOD LISTENS
NOT TO YOUR
WORDS SAVE
WHEN HE
HIMSELF UTTERS
THEM THROUGH
YOUR LIPS.

AND I CANNOT TEACH YOU THE PRAYER OF THE SEAS AND THE FORESTS AND THE MOUNTAINS. BUT YOU WHO ARE BORN OF THE MOUNTAINS AND THE FORESTS AND THE SEAS CAN FIND THEIR PRAYER IN YOUR HEART,

AND IF YOU BUT LISTEN IN THE STILLNESS OF THE NIGHT YOU SHALL HEAR THEM SAYING IN SILENCE:

"OUR GOD, WHO ART OUR WINGED SELF, IT IS THY WILL IN US THAT WILLETH.
IT IS THY DESIRE IN US THAT DESIRETH.
IT IS THY URGE IN US THAT WOULD TURN OUR NIGHTS, WHICH ARE THINE, INTO DAYS, WHICH ARE THINE ALSO.
WE CANNOT ASK THEE FOR AUGHT, FOR THOU KNOWEST OUR NEEDS BEFORE THEY ARE BORN IN US:
THOU ART OUR NEED; AND IN GIVING US MORE OF THYSELF THOU GIVEST US ALL."

AND AN OLD PRIEST SAID,
SPEAK TO US OF RELIGION.

AND HE SAID:

HAVE I SPOKEN THIS DAY OF
AUGHT ELSE?

IS NOT RELIGION ALL DEEDS
AND ALL REFLECTION,
AND THAT WHICH IS NEITHER
DEED NOR REFLECTION, BUT
A WONDER AND A SURPRISE
EVER SPRINGING IN THE SOUL,
EVEN WHILE THE HANDS HEW
THE STONE OR TEND THE
LOOM?

WHO CAN SEPARATE HIS
FAITH FROM HIS ACTIONS,
OR HIS BELIEF FROM HIS
OCCUPATIONS?

WHO CAN SPREAD HIS HOURS
BEFORE HIM, SAYING, "THIS
FOR GOD AND THIS FOR
MYSELF; THIS FOR MY SOUL,
AND THIS OTHER FOR MY
BODY"?

ALL YOUR HOURS ARE WINGS
THAT BEAT THROUGH SPACE
FROM SELF TO SELF.

HE WHO WEARS HIS MORALITY
BUT AS HIS BEST GARMENT
WERE BETTER NAKED.
THE WIND AND THE SUN WILL
TEAR NO HOLES IN HIS SKIN.

AND HE WHO DEFINES
HIS CONDUCT BY ETHICS
IMPRISONS HIS SONG-BIRD IN
A CAGE.
THE FREEST SONG COMES
NOT THROUGH BARS AND
WIRES.

AND HE TO WHOM
WORSHIPPING IS A WINDOW,
TO OPEN BUT ALSO TO SHUT,
HAS NOT YET VISITED THE
HOUSE OF HIS SOUL WHOSE
WINDOWS ARE FROM DAWN
TO DAWN.

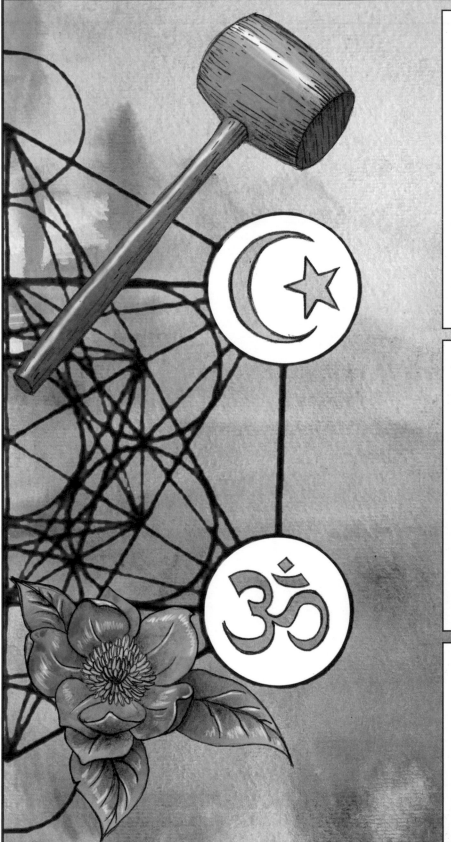

YOUR DAILY LIFE IS YOUR TEMPLE AND YOUR RELIGION.

WHENEVER YOU ENTER INTO IT TAKE WITH YOU YOUR ALL.

TAKE THE PLOUGH AND THE FORGE AND THE MALLET AND THE LUTE, THE THINGS YOU HAVE FASHIONED IN NECESSITY OR FOR DELIGHT.

FOR IN REVERIE YOU CANNOT RISE ABOVE YOUR ACHIEVEMENTS NOR FALL LOWER THAN YOUR FAILURES.

AND TAKE WITH YOU ALL MEN:
FOR IN ADORATION YOU CANNOT FLY HIGHER THAN THEIR HOPES NOR HUMBLE YOURSELF LOWER THAN THEIR DESPAIR.

AND IF YOU WOULD KNOW GOD BE NOT THEREFORE A SOLVER OF RIDDLES.

RATHER LOOK ABOUT YOU AND YOU SHALL SEE HIM PLAYING WITH YOUR CHILDREN.

AND LOOK INTO SPACE; YOU SHALL SEE HIM WALKING IN THE CLOUD, OUTSTRETCHING HIS ARMS IN THE LIGHTNING AND DESCENDING IN RAIN.

YOU SHALL SEE HIM SMILING IN FLOWERS, THEN RISING AND WAVING HIS HANDS IN TREES.

THEN ALMITRA SPOKE, SAYING: WE WOULD ASK NOW OF DEATH.

AND HE SAID:

YOU WOULD KNOW THE SECRET OF DEATH.

BUT HOW SHALL YOU FIND IT UNLESS YOU SEEK IT IN THE HEART OF LIFE?

THE OWL WHOSE NIGHT-BOUND EYES ARE BLIND UNTO THE DAY CANNOT UNVEIL THE MYSTERY OF LIGHT.

IF YOU WOULD INDEED BEHOLD THE SPIRIT OF DEATH, OPEN YOUR HEART WIDE UNTO THE BODY OF LIFE.

FOR LIFE AND DEATH ARE ONE, EVEN AS THE RIVER AND THE SEA ARE ONE.

IN THE DEPTH OF YOUR HOPES AND DESIRES LIES YOUR SILENT KNOWLEDGE OF THE BEYOND; AND LIKE SEEDS DREAMING BENEATH THE SNOW YOUR HEART DREAMS OF SPRING.

TRUST THE DREAMS, FOR IN THEM IS HIDDEN THE GATE TO ETERNITY.

YOUR FEAR OF DEATH IS BUT THE TREMBLING OF THE SHEPHERD WHEN HE STANDS BEFORE THE KING WHOSE HAND IS TO BE LAID UPON HIM IN HONOUR.

IS THE SHEPHERD NOT JOYFUL BENEATH HIS TREMBLING, THAT HE SHALL WEAR THE MARK OF THE KING?

YET IS HE NOT MORE MINDFUL OF HIS TREMBLING?

FOR WHAT IS IT TO DIE BUT TO STAND NAKED IN THE WIND AND TO MELT INTO THE SUN?

AND WHAT IS IT TO CEASE BREATHING, BUT TO FREE THE BREATH FROM ITS RESTLESS TIDES, THAT IT MAY RISE AND EXPAND AND SEEK GOD UNENCUMBERED?

ONLY WHEN YOU DRINK FROM THE RIVER OF SILENCE SHALL YOU INDEED SING.

AND WHEN YOU HAVE REACHED THE MOUNTAIN TOP, THEN YOU SHALL BEGIN TO CLIMB.

AND WHEN THE EARTH SHALL CLAIM YOUR LIMBS, THEN SHALL YOU TRULY DANCE.

105

AND NOW IT WAS EVENING.

BLESSED BE THIS DAY AND THIS PLACE AND YOUR SPIRIT THAT HAS SPOKEN.

WAS IT I WHO SPOKE? WAS I NOT ALSO A LISTENER?

THEN HE DESCENDED THE STEPS OF THE TEMPLE AND ALL THE PEOPLE FOLLOWED HIM. AND HE REACHED HIS SHIP AND STOOD UPON THE DECK.

AND FACING THE PEOPLE AGAIN, HE RAISED HIS VOICE AND SAID:

PEOPLE OF ORPHALESE, THE WIND BIDS ME LEAVE YOU.

LESS HASTY AM I THAN THE WIND, YET I MUST GO.

WE WANDERERS, EVER SEEKING THE LONELIER WAY, BEGIN NO DAY WHERE WE HAVE ENDED ANOTHER DAY; AND NO SUNRISE FINDS US WHERE SUNSET LEFT US.

EVEN WHILE THE EARTH SLEEPS, WE TRAVEL.

WE ARE THE SEEDS OF THE TENACIOUS PLANT, AND IT IS IN OUR RIPENESS AND OUR FULLNESS OF HEART THAT WE ARE GIVEN TO THE WIND AND ARE SCATTERED.

BRIEF WERE MY DAYS AMONG YOU, AND BRIEFER STILL THE WORDS I HAVE SPOKEN.

BUT SHOULD MY VOICE FADE IN YOUR EARS, AND MY LOVE VANISH IN YOUR MEMORY, THEN I WILL COME AGAIN, AND WITH A RICHER HEART AND LIPS MORE YIELDING TO THE SPIRIT WILL I SPEAK.

YEA, I SHALL RETURN WITH THE TIDE, AND THOUGH DEATH MAY HIDE ME, AND THE GREATER SILENCE ENFOLD ME, YET AGAIN WILL I SEEK YOUR UNDERSTANDING.

AND NOT IN VAIN WILL I SEEK.

IF AUGHT I HAVE SAID IS TRUTH, THAT TRUTH SHALL REVEAL ITSELF IN A CLEARER VOICE, AND IN WORDS MORE KIN TO YOUR THOUGHTS.

I GO WITH THE WIND, PEOPLE OF ORPHALESE, BUT NOT DOWN INTO EMPTINESS; AND IF THIS DAY IS NOT A FULFILMENT OF YOUR NEEDS AND MY LOVE, THEN LET IT BE A PROMISE TILL ANOTHER DAY.

MAN'S NEEDS CHANGE, BUT NOT HIS LOVE, NOR HIS DESIRE THAT HIS LOVE SHOULD SATISFY HIS NEEDS.

KNOW THEREFORE, THAT FROM THE GREATER SILENCE I SHALL RETURN.

THE MIST THAT DRIFTS AWAY AT DAWN, LEAVING BUT DEW IN THE FIELDS, SHALL RISE AND GATHER INTO A CLOUD AND THEN FALL DOWN IN RAIN.

AND NOT UNLIKE THE MIST HAVE I BEEN.

IN THE STILLNESS OF THE NIGHT I HAVE WALKED IN YOUR STREETS, AND MY SPIRIT HAS ENTERED YOUR HOUSES,

AND YOUR HEART-BEATS WERE IN MY HEART, AND YOUR BREATH WAS UPON MY FACE, AND I KNEW YOU ALL.

AY, I KNEW YOUR JOY AND YOUR PAIN, AND IN YOUR SLEEP YOUR DREAMS WERE MY DREAMS.

AND OFTENTIMES I WAS AMONG YOU A LAKE AMONG THE MOUNTAINS.

I MIRRORED THE SUMMITS IN YOU AND THE BENDING SLOPES, AND EVEN THE PASSING FLOCKS OF YOUR THOUGHTS AND YOUR DESIRES.

AND TO MY SILENCE CAME THE LAUGHTER OF YOUR CHILDREN IN STREAMS, AND THE LONGING OF YOUR YOUTHS IN RIVERS.

AND WHEN THEY REACHED MY DEPTH THE STREAMS AND THE RIVERS CEASED NOT YET TO SING.

113

AND LIKE THE SEASONS YOU ARE ALSO,
AND THOUGH IN YOUR WINTER YOU DENY YOUR SPRING,

YET SPRING, REPOSING WITHIN YOU, SMILES IN HER DROWSINESS AND IS NOT OFFENDED.

THINK NOT I SAY THESE THINGS IN ORDER THAT YOU MAY SAY THE ONE TO THE OTHER, "HE PRAISED US WELL. HE SAW BUT THE GOOD IN US."

I ONLY SPEAK TO YOU IN WORDS OF THAT WHICH YOU YOURSELVES KNOW IN THOUGHT.

AND WHAT IS WORD KNOWLEDGE BUT A SHADOW OF WORDLESS KNOWLEDGE?

YOUR THOUGHTS AND MY WORDS ARE WAVES FROM A SEALED MEMORY THAT KEEPS RECORDS OF OUR YESTERDAYS,

AND OF THE ANCIENT DAYS WHEN THE EARTH KNEW NOT US NOR HERSELF,

AND OF NIGHTS WHEN EARTH WAS UPWROUGHT WITH CONFUSION.

WISE MEN HAVE COME TO YOU TO GIVE YOU OF THEIR WISDOM. I CAME TO TAKE OF YOUR WISDOM:

AND BEHOLD I HAVE FOUND THAT WHICH IS GREATER THAN WISDOM.

IT IS A FLAME SPIRIT IN YOU EVER GATHERING MORE OF ITSELF,
WHILE YOU, HEEDLESS OF ITS EXPANSION, BEWAIL THE WITHERING OF YOUR DAYS.

IT IS LIFE IN QUEST OF LIFE IN BODIES THAT FEAR THE GRAVE.

THERE ARE NO GRAVES HERE.

THESE MOUNTAINS AND PLAINS ARE A CRADLE AND A STEPPING-STONE.

WHENEVER YOU PASS BY THE FIELD WHERE YOU HAVE LAID YOUR ANCESTORS LOOK WELL THEREUPON, AND YOU SHALL SEE YOURSELVES AND YOUR CHILDREN DANCING HAND IN HAND.

VERILY YOU OFTEN MAKE MERRY WITHOUT KNOWING.

OTHERS HAVE COME TO YOU TO WHOM FOR GOLDEN PROMISES MADE UNTO YOUR FAITH YOU HAVE GIVEN BUT RICHES AND POWER AND GLORY.

LESS THAN A PROMISE HAVE I GIVEN, AND YET MORE GENEROUS HAVE YOU BEEN TO ME.

YOU HAVE GIVEN ME MY DEEPER THIRSTING AFTER LIFE.

SURELY THERE IS NO GREATER GIFT TO A MAN THAN THAT WHICH TURNS ALL HIS AIMS INTO PARCHING LIPS AND ALL LIFE INTO A FOUNTAIN.

AND IN THIS LIES MY HONOUR AND MY REWARD--

THAT WHENEVER I COME TO THE FOUNTAIN TO DRINK I FIND THE LIVING WATER ITSELF THIRSTY;

AND IT DRINKS ME WHILE I DRINK IT.

SOME OF YOU HAVE DEEMED ME PROUD AND OVER-SHY TO RECEIVE GIFTS.
TOO PROUD INDEED AM I TO RECEIVE WAGES, BUT NOT GIFTS.

AND THOUGH I HAVE EATEN BERRIES AMONG THE HILLS WHEN YOU WOULD HAVE HAD ME SIT AT YOUR BOARD, AND SLEPT IN THE PORTICO OF THE TEMPLE WHEN YOU WOULD GLADLY HAVE SHELTERED ME, YET IT WAS NOT YOUR LOVING MINDFULNESS OF MY DAYS AND MY NIGHTS THAT MADE FOOD SWEET TO MY MOUTH AND GIRDLED MY SLEEP WITH VISIONS?

FOR THIS I BLESS YOU MOST:

YOU GIVE MUCH AND KNOW NOT THAT YOU GIVE AT ALL. VERILY THE KINDNESS THAT GAZES UPON ITSELF IN A MIRROR TURNS TO STONE, AND A GOOD DEED THAT CALLS ITSELF BY TENDER NAMES BECOMES THE PARENT TO A CURSE.

AND SOME OF YOU HAVE CALLED ME ALOOF, AND DRUNK WITH MY OWN ALONENESS, AND YOU HAVE SAID, "HE HOLDS COUNCIL WITH THE TREES OF THE FOREST, BUT NOT WITH MEN. HE SITS ALONE ON HILL-TOPS AND LOOKS DOWN UPON OUR CITY."

TRUE IT IS THAT I HAVE CLIMBED THE HILLS AND WALKED IN REMOTE PLACES.

HOW COULD I HAVE SEEN YOU SAVE FROM A GREAT HEIGHT OR A GREAT DISTANCE?

HOW CAN ONE BE INDEED NEAR UNLESS HE BE FAR?

AND OTHERS AMONG YOU CALLED UNTO ME, NOT IN WORDS, AND THEY SAID:

"STRANGER, STRANGER, LOVER OF UNREACHABLE HEIGHTS, WHY DWELL YOU AMONG THE SUMMITS WHERE EAGLES BUILD THEIR NESTS?
WHY SEEK YOU THE UNATTAINABLE?
WHAT STORMS WOULD YOU TRAP IN YOUR NET,
AND WHAT VAPOROUS BIRDS DO YOU HUNT IN THE SKY?
COME AND BE ONE OF US.
DESCEND AND APPEASE YOUR HUNGER WITH OUR BREAD AND QUENCH YOUR THIRST WITH OUR WINE."

IN THE SOLITUDE OF THEIR SOULS THEY SAID THESE THINGS;

BUT WERE THEIR SOLITUDE DEEPER THEY WOULD HAVE KNOWN THAT I SOUGHT BUT THE SECRET OF YOUR JOY AND YOUR PAIN,
AND I HUNTED ONLY YOUR LARGER SELVES THAT WALK THE SKY.

BUT THE HUNTER WAS ALSO THE HUNTED;

FOR MANY OF MY ARROWS LEFT MY BOW ONLY TO SEEK MY OWN BREAST.

AND THE FLIER WAS ALSO THE CREEPER;
FOR WHEN MY WINGS WERE SPREAD IN THE SUN THEIR SHADOW UPON THE EARTH WAS A TURTLE.

AND I THE BELIEVER WAS ALSO THE DOUBTER;
FOR OFTEN HAVE I PUT MY FINGER IN MY OWN WOUND THAT I MIGHT HAVE THE GREATER BELIEF IN YOU AND THE GREATER KNOWLEDGE OF YOU.

121

BUT NOW OUR SLEEP HAS FLED AND OUR DREAM IS OVER, AND IT IS NO LONGER DAWN.

THE NOONTIDE IS UPON US AND OUR HALF WAKING HAS TURNED TO FULLER DAY, AND WE MUST PART.

IF IN THE TWILIGHT OF MEMORY WE SHOULD MEET ONCE MORE, WE SHALL SPEAK AGAIN TOGETHER AND YOU SHALL SING TO ME A DEEPER SONG.

AND IF OUR HANDS SHOULD MEET IN ANOTHER DREAM WE SHALL BUILD ANOTHER TOWER IN THE SKY.

SO SAYING HE MADE A SIGNAL TO THE SEAMEN, AND STRAIGHTAWAY THEY WEIGHED ANCHOR AND CAST THE SHIP LOOSE FROM ITS MOORINGS, AND THEY MOVED EASTWARD.

AND A CRY CAME FROM THE PEOPLE AS FROM A SINGLE HEART, AND IT ROSE INTO THE DUSK AND WAS CARRIED OUT OVER THE SEA LIKE A GREAT TRUMPETING.

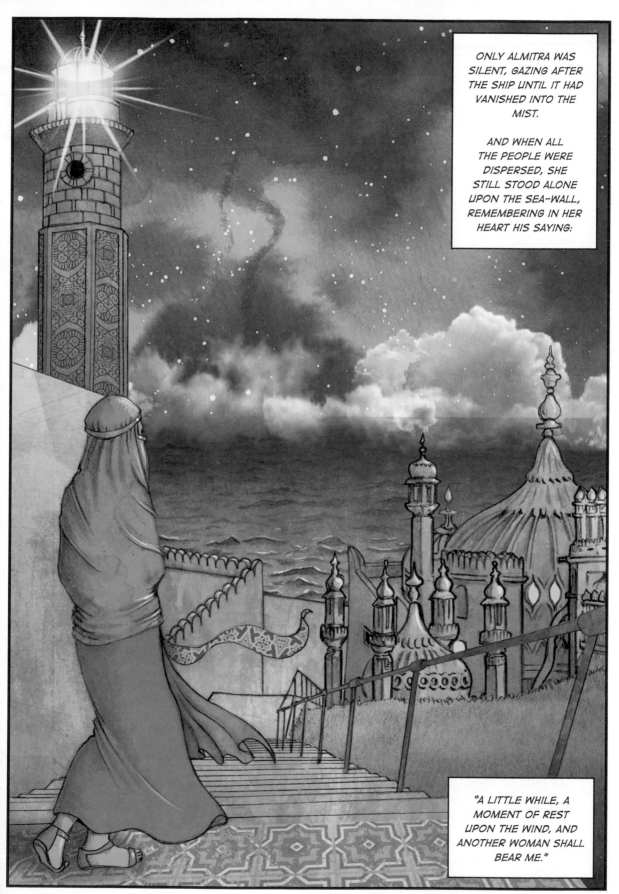

ONLY ALMITRA WAS SILENT, GAZING AFTER THE SHIP UNTIL IT HAD VANISHED INTO THE MIST.

AND WHEN ALL THE PEOPLE WERE DISPERSED, SHE STILL STOOD ALONE UPON THE SEA-WALL, REMEMBERING IN HER HEART HIS SAYING:

"A LITTLE WHILE, A MOMENT OF REST UPON THE WIND, AND ANOTHER WOMAN SHALL BEAR ME."

SOME TIME LATER...

126

Acknowledgments

This book is dedicated to the courageous medical professionals and key workers who battle on the front lines against the coronavirus all over the world on humanity's behalf. There are no words strong enough for our gratitude.

Thank you to Paul Mayor, for supporting me and putting up with me. Especially while I'm in "book mode." I couldn't do it without you. For Ma, Cos, and Ruth, for their constant love and unwavering support. I would like to thank the people kind enough to model for me: Andrew Casey, Rebecca Hull, Rod Connolly, Mark O'Neill, Ahmed Jay, and Alex Feeney. Sending big love and appreciation to my family and friends who I don't get to see often enough.

To my family: Kev and Francie, Colin and Colette, Darren, Damien and Lorraine, Aisling and Cahal, Niamh and Stuart, Mikey, Phillip and Aideen, Mike and Mary, Tommy and Evelyn, and of course all the kids who I don't have space to list! Corrie, Debbie and Shaun, Jacques and Charlie. To my friends: Andrew Casey, Nick Jackson, Stephen Pearce, Rebecca Hull, Sebastian Cheswright Cater, Maxine Doyle, Ben Vincent, Keith Davie, Laura Thomas, Jon King, and all the Aberdare gang, Alex and Steph, Han and Karolien, Simon Hayward, Jon Byrne, Bill and Vicky, Paul Ryan, Jo Lloyd, Adam and Mari, the Reckless Records crew, and finally all the gang from Brighton.

About the artist and author

Pete Katz is a half-Irish/half-Greek illustrator and writer, born in the East End of London. He has been a freelance illustrator for almost twenty years and has worked for clients including Oxfam, Barnes & Noble, Le Monde, Image Comics, Scholastic, and the British Museum. This is the seventh graphic novel he has produced. *The Art of War* (2018) is also available from Canterbury Classics. More of his work can be found at inkandmanners.com or @nutkin on Instagram.